MIRRORS & WINDOWS

MIRRORS & WINDOWS

BY ROSIE BAKER

NEW DEGREE PRESS
COPYRIGHT © 2020 ROSIE BAKER
All rights reserved.

MIRRORS & WINDOWS

ISBN
978-1-64137-975-5   *Paperback*
978-1-64137-857-4   *Kindle Ebook*
978-1-64137-858-1   *Digital Ebook*

To my family: Mum, Dad, Beth, and Nanna. Thank you for your constant love and for believing in me right from the beginning when I told you about the opportunity to write a book. And to Brandon, for your encouragement to write every night even after a long day.

CONTENTS

—

	INTRODUCTION	9
CHAPTER 1	TIME FOR SOME CHANGE	15
CHAPTER 2	DR. G IS LIVING HER DREAM	23
CHAPTER 3	SHERYL SANDBERG IS LEANING IN	33
CHAPTER 4	BELIEVING IN YOURSELF WITH SUSAN O'DAY	43
CHAPTER 5	GAY COOK AND LIFE'S SERIES OF EVENTS	53
CHAPTER 6	ALL YOU NEED IS LOVE AND JACKIE SPENCER TO SHOW YOU THE SIGHTS	63
CHAPTER 7	SUSAN SANTNER AND THE IMPORTANCE OF BEING HAPPY IN YOUR JOB	71
CHAPTER 8	BUILDING HUNDREDS OF MIRRORS WITH DEBRA BENTON	81
CHAPTER 9	JUDITH HEUMANN'S FIGHT FOR CHANGE	93
CHAPTER 10	VISUALIZATION AND ITS POWER	103
CHAPTER 11	YOUR DREAM CAN BE A REALITY	111
CHAPTER 12	THE MAGIC BEGINS IN PENCILS	119
CHAPTER 13	OPRAH WINFREY AND VISION BOARDS	129
	CONCLUSION	137
	APPENDIX	143
	ACKNOWLEDGMENTS	149

INTRODUCTION

When women are asked to reveal their dreams, they are rarely asked how they will make them happen. As preschoolers, little girls are asked what they want to be when they grow up. High school teens are challenged to determine a university major by the age of seventeen, and young university girls are asked what they will do after graduation. Typically, women, including myself and others I know, are told in response to dream bigger. This raises the question: how do we make a dream a reality?

This question resonates with many of us, no matter what gender. Is it possible for everyone to make their dreams a reality, or do only a select, lucky few have success stories to tell?

I believe we all can make our dreams a reality. I've included the success stories of others in this book, *Mirrors & Windows*, as reflections of who we can be. It starts with envisioning what we wish to accomplish. Then each day, we can practice a way to manifest and envision those dreams to make them a reality.

I started writing this book because I wanted to discover the power of vision and the power of putting this vision into practice. If we can change the way we think and what we think, we can open up endless possibilities. Part of envisioning is observing and learning from the stories of successful women who can serve as mentors for us all.

According to *Forbes Magazine*, mentoring has many positive benefits.[1] "For individuals, studies show that good mentoring can lead to greater career success, including promotions, raises, and increased opportunities. Organizations that embrace mentoring are rewarded with higher levels of employee engagement, retention, and knowledge sharing. In fact, mentoring has proved so beneficial that 71 percent of Fortune 500 companies offer mentoring programs to their employees."[2]

Mentoring expert Drew Appleby, PhD, professor emeritus at Indiana University-Purdue University Indianapolis, says, "Mentors are crucial whenever people are faced with new phases of their career or life that require the development of new knowledge, skills or attitudes."[3] Having mentors helps others work out who they want to be along with how they must change to become their desired person and how they can take advantage of opportunities offered to them. Mentors and role models can be our mirrors and guides when facing new challenges in our lives.[4]

---

[1] Mary Abbajay, "Mentoring Matters: Three Essential Elements of Success," *Forbes Magazine*, Jan 20, 2019.

[2] Ibid.

[3] Heather Stringer, "The Life-Changing Power of Mentors," *American Psychological Association* 47, no.6. (June 2016): 54.

[4] Ibid.

Forbes Magazine writes that, although it takes work and time, having a mentor is one of the "most important things a person can do to enhance their career and professional life."[5] When used correctly, mentoring can provide success to both the mentee and the mentor.

We've all had people influence our lives and become role models and mentors. They might have been friends, family members, teachers, or even much-loved celebrities. I realize just how much I have been positively affected by role models and mentors throughout my life. This has made me ask an important question: do we need role models and mentors to be successful?

Identifying as a woman, I also wanted to explore stories of other females who dreamed and achieved success. In many of the stories I followed, the women did not have concrete role models or someone who physically resembled them in their targeted career field. Instead, they used windows to envision their futures, and they are now the mirror for others to reflect upon today. In this book, you will discover the stories of successful women like Sheryl Sandberg, Ashanti Johnson, and Dr. Aidyl Gonzalez-Serricchio (Dr. G), who all created their own visions or windows and were successful in doing so.

These women's success stories raised further questions for me. Are these inspiring, real women unique or part of a larger trend? Do they all share something in common? After talking to them and hearing their stories, I found something that changed the way I see the future of success.

---

5   Mary Abbajay, "Mentoring Matters: Three Essential Elements of Success," *Forbes Magazine,* Jan 20, 2019.

I felt compelled to write this book because I wanted to explore the power of vision, which I visualize as windows, and the importance of having role models and mentors, or mirrors in our lives. My own experiences as a young woman going to university and beginning my career along with interviewing many successful women in this book have given me empowering insights.

Since the beginning of freshman year at university, I have been a writer in a nationwide club called Her Campus, currently with approximately 320 chapters in forty-four states and nine countries involving more than ten thousand contributors. *Her Campus* is an online magazine, and each chapter writes and uploads articles and performs many other activities like organizing campuswide events for International Women's Day in March every year.

Being part of this organization has allowed me to meet many amazing young women from my campus from all over America. Their drive and tenacity have inspired me and pushed me closer to achieving my goals.

This book should be read by those who are:

- Currently in high school or university

- Starting a career

- Wanting a change in career

- Inspired to achieve a dream or goal

Reading this book will:

- Inspire you

- Encourage you to embrace changes

- Challenge you to set new goals and achieve them

- Help you mirror the success of others

- Assist you in the practice of envisioning in day-to-day life

- Open you to insights to improve your mindset

It is my hope that this book will make a difference in the lives of all who read it.

CHAPTER 1

TIME FOR SOME CHANGE

One of my favorite quotes is from the Disney film *Ratatouille*, when Remy the rat says, "The only thing predictable about life is its unpredictability."[6] Change in our lives is inevitable as the days, weeks, months, and years pass. Yet we often find change difficult, and many of us may even hide or avoid certain things that we know will bring change into our lives.

Santosh Kesari, MD, PhD, neurologist, neuro-oncologist, and neuroscientist, explained that change is often difficult, whether we're going on a new diet or starting a new job, because our brains are trying to protect us from something that could be dangerous.[7] When we're young, our brains are "figuring out positive and negative behaviors, what is good for survival, and avoiding consequences that would cause even short-term pain. As we age, our brain learns ways to do things that make us do certain things and behave accordingly

---

[6] Rachel Berman, "Super Deep Disney Quotes | Movies," *Oh My Disney*, accessed May 17, 2020.

[7] Nicole Spector, "Why We Find Change So Difficult, According to Neuroscience," *NBC News*, accessed November 12, 2018.

to each context and each stimulus."[8] This is good and bad news. It's good news because we learn positive behaviors and remember them and bad news when we want to learn new behaviors.

When we change something, our brains think we could be doing something potentially threatening. "From an evolutionary standpoint we develop these neural pathways to adapt to live, so when we encounter change, our brain shifts into a protective mode," said Dr. Sanam Hafeez, a licensed clinical psychologist and neuropsychologist.[9] "It has to use energy from reserves and it doesn't know, from that evolutionary standpoint, if the change is good for us or not. It doesn't know if this change is a one-time deal or whether it needs to re-establish a routine. 'Will it hurt me?' A lot of red flags go up."[10]

Therefore, fearing change or feeling stressed out about it is only natural. This is why teaching our brains to get used to change is important. Just like training our bodies in a gym, we can train our brains. To do this, we need to step out of our comfort zones and have new experiences.

STEPPING OUT OF THE COMFORT ZONE
We've all experienced the stress of change. I know I certainly have. In fact, I've had a crash course in change and stepping outside my comfort zone. In 2015, I moved from a small village in southern England to one of the world's busiest and most

---

8   Ibid.
9   Ibid.
10 Ibid.

vibrant cities, Los Angeles, California. I dove headfirst into a brand-new culture. I adapted to attending an American high school with baseball games and yellow school buses and to a university with homecoming and dorm living. I did this while making lifelong friends who have different traditions and a different vocabulary, like "sweater" instead of "jumper." Let's not forget the other little pieces that come with moving to a new country that aren't spelled out in a guidebook. It's like one giant puzzle you never quite complete even when you think you've found the last piece.

We've all had moments that require taking that first, nerve-wracking step—whether that is the first day of university, applying for a new job, or breaking up with someone. Often, you can mentally prepare for these times because you've anticipated them and you've spent time thinking about what is behind the door. When I started university, I spent the summer before watching as many YouTube videos as I could about living on a college campus. I read books about life hacks and spoke to friends who had already spent a year at university away from home to help prepare me for this change.

I know that change can be scary. I like to think of it as the "what's behind the door" moment in a horror movie. We all know what we face when looking at the metaphorical door, but we don't know what lies behind it. The unknown and the anxiety build when thinking about what lies behind it. Sometimes the actual change isn't the overwhelming part, but instead the anxiety that comes with the unknown. However, if we want to face it, we must open the door and take the first step into the other side.

We can easily get stuck in our day-to-day lives. We like our routines because we feel safe. We have programmed ourselves to feel safe with what we know. We feel comfortable. But that is the damaging part. It is more damaging for us to not step outside of our comfort zones to find change.

Before I started my first day of high school in LA, I was required or highly encouraged to partake in a four-day outdoor education trip canoeing twenty miles down the Russian River in Northern California. This was an eleven-hour coach journey with total strangers. I remember lying in bed in the middle of the night staring at the packed suitcase on the floor. Every part of my body was screaming at me not to go. I had only met a handful of peers when touring the school a few days prior. Other than that, I was going on the trip not knowing anyone.

Four days later when I arrived in the high school car park in the dark of the night, I'm pretty sure I stepped off the coach beaming from ear to ear. For a small village English girl, I'd just had the adventure of a lifetime. Not knowing anyone was hard and scary, but also amazing. I had made friends (who would become my best friends), I had seen my first shooting star while camping outside in my sleeping bag, and I had proven myself to be stronger physically, emotionally, and mentally then I ever thought I was.

I felt my confidence boost from this trip after learning so much about myself in a short period. If I had not decided to go, I would never have had these experiences and incredible memories to look back on. When we fail to step outside of our comfort zones and embrace change, we stop ourselves from growing. We stop ourselves from opportunities that can grow our characters and shape us.

I liked to avoid change before I moved across the pond. I had my routines and comfort zones, thinking they were all I needed. Honestly, I was scared of change, and many of us are. I still am. But fast forward a few years later, and I have a new perspective. I value change and stepping outside my comfort zone. I'm not a wild child or a risk taker, but I understand the importance of stepping outside of our comfort zones and trying new things that make us feel uncomfortable.

Debra Benton, who we will meet later in the book, is a good example of a woman who embraced a sudden change and turned it into an opportunity that later shaped her life. At twenty-three years old, she was fired from a special management trainee program at a computer company. The reason why? Her boss decided she didn't get along well with men. She took this sudden change as an opportunity to learn. If she had not been fired, she would not have worked on herself or had a very successful career coaching CEOs and leaders around the world.

If you are given the opportunity to grow and to strengthen your character when you step out of your comfort zone, why not take the chance to do it? Even if it makes you feel uncomfortable because it is new and different, imagine how proud you'll feel after you have accomplished it. Some change is out of our control, such as what happened to Debra, but that does not mean it won't lead us to good things. Not all change is bad. Remember that "a comfort zone is a beautiful place, but nothing ever grows there."[11]

---

[11] "A Comfort Zone Is a Beautiful Place, But Nothing Ever Grows There. (With Images) | Comfort Zone Quotes, Boxing Quotes, Life Quotes," *Pinterest*, accessed May 17, 2020.

CREATING CHANGE

There have been hundreds, if not thousands, of inspirational stories of women who have embraced and created change. Think of Emmeline Pankhurst, a fearless suffragette whose efforts allowed some women to vote in 1918.[12] What about Hattie McDaniel, the first African American actor to win an Oscar in 1940?[13] Jane Fonda, an actress, activist, and an inspiration for others in her generation helped people look after their fitness and health.[14] Princess Diana gave society a voice by working with various charities to support AIDS.[15] Lastly, Emma Watson, who not only plays one of the world's most beloved characters, Hermione Granger in *Harry Potter,* is also outspoken about feminism and is not afraid to voice concern.[16]

Although change and comfort zones are two different concepts, they are closely related. Without stepping outside your comfort zone, how will you reach your dreams and make that change happen? Malala Yousafzai is a great example of someone who wanted to create change and did so incredibly successfully.[17]

When Malala was ten in 2007, the Taliban began controlling Swat Valley, Pakistan, where she lived. Girls were banned from

---

12   Jenny Proudfoot, "The 100 Most Inspirational Women of the Last 100 Years," *Marie Claire,* uploaded March 5, 2020.

13   "Hattie Mcdaniel – IMDB," accessed May 17, 2020.

14   Jenny Proudfoot, "The 100 Most Inspirational Women of the Last 100 Years," *Marie Claire,* uploaded March 5, 2020.

15   Ibid.

16   Ibid.

17   "The Nobel Peace Prize 2014," *Nobel Prize,* accessed May 17, 2020.

attending school and even participating in cultural activities such as dancing. Malala disagreed with what was happening and used her voice anonymously to talk to the media and the BBC about it. For the next three years, she worked with her father to campaign for her right to go to school and for other Pakistani girls to have free access to quality education. In 2011, she was nominated for the International Children's Peace Prize. However, on October 9, 2012, fifteen-year-old Malala was shot by the Taliban on a bus heading home from school.

She was injured badly but survived after being taken to hospital in Birmingham, England, where she amazingly made a full recovery. Afterward, she continued her education in England and later went on to study at Oxford University. When she was sixteen years old, she wrote a biography about her journey called *I Am Malala: The Girl Who Stood Up for Education and Was Shot by the Taliban*.[18] At just seventeen years old, she cofounded the Malala Fund with her father "to give back to girls what poverty, war, and discrimination tried to take away."[19] On top of everything, in 2014, she also became the youngest person to receive a Nobel Peace Prize.

Although incredibly young, Malala has achieved so much and changed lives across the world. After being thrown into a major life change, she saw it as an opportunity to do something good and a way to make something happen. Change can come unexpectedly, and it is not always good, but you can control the outcome. You get to write your story! Malala

---

18 Ibid.

19 "Malala Fund | Working for a World Where All Girls Can Learn and Lead," *Malala.Org*, accessed May 17, 2020.

shows that you are capable of anything when you put your mind to it. Her story, along with her courage and determination, serves an inspiration to millions across the world.

LESSONS FROM THIS CHAPTER:

- Embrace change.

- Step outside your comfort zone.

- Don't let being scared of change or feeling uncomfortable outside your comfort zone stop you from achieving your dreams and goals.

- Use visualization to help you feel more confident about stepping into change and outside your comfort zones.

- Learn from and mirror the successes of others.

CHAPTER 2

DR. G IS LIVING HER DREAM

Dr. G is one of my mirrors.

Aidyl Gonzalez-Serricchio is creating change and has been stepping out of comfort zones her whole life. Her love for science started when she was about five years old. While getting ready for school one morning, she spotted a cockroach beneath the window laying eggs in her two-bedroom Bronx apartment. She decided to hide some of the eggs in a shoebox, away from her parents, brother, and sister. After that day, it became her routine to check on them every morning when getting ready for school, as she wanted to see if anything would happen to them.

As it turns out, something did happen. She watched them hatch into little larvae before growing into small cockroaches. When first hatched, they were white before turning a darker color. Amazed at her discovery of their transformation, she went to tell her mother about what she had found. At first, her mother was confused about how she knew all this information. When she learned about the shoe box, she immediately started telling her off and told her to go kill the roaches. Aidyl gently laughed next to me as she reminisced on the story that sparked the inspiration of her love of science. Little did her five-year-old self know that moment would influence the rest of her life and her intrigue would grow more passionate as the years passed.

"I want to never forget how beautiful science is when you experience it the first time," she explained, looking serious and passionate. "I always wanted to make sure I had those fresh eyes. It's just four little chemicals that make us, you know, and that's the reason.... Whatever your background or your capabilities or your quirkiness, it doesn't restrict you from anything you want to do, because I hate it when people said I couldn't without a reason."

Known as Dr. G on her high school campus, she is loved by many of her students. She has sparked interest and intrigue in students over the years, which inspired them to go to college and study. She is captivating to watch. Her personality is infectious, and her students get caught up in her enthusiasm. She moves like a small whirlwind. Like a five-foot-tall, petite-framed energizer bunny, she seems ready to take on anything the day throws at her.

Dr. G holds many titles. She has several roles at the Buckley School in Los Angeles. She is the science department cochair, science, technology, engineering, and mathematics (STEM) director, high school teacher, and robotics director. Although science is considered Dr. G's main passion, she has many others, including being a magician at the prestigious Magic Castle in Hollywood. In addition, she is a science astronaut in training to take samples from clouds in the mesosphere.

When I visited Dr. G on campus, it was not an unusual Saturday morning for her. With her hair pulled back into a ponytail, her thick Bronx, Latina accent carried itself through the classroom as she talked to her students. She was working in her high school classroom, helping her students with their experiments and research. Moving around with ease, she was looking for equipment stored away in the cupboards while explaining to the students what they needed to do and how to do it. One wall of the classroom was lined with fish tanks while others had posters tacked to them explaining different scientific concepts. In the corner of the classroom stood a skeleton on wheels that my classmates used to love messing with.

DR. G'S FIGHT FOR CHANGE

It has not been an easy journey for Dr. G to be where she is today as an accomplished scientist, professor, and mother. She grew up in the Bronx in New York, scared that anytime a loved one left the house, she would never see them again because her neighborhood was riddled with crime. She was told she couldn't go to university when in high school and that she would not be successful.

When she was in her early thirties, she was nearly paralyzed for life due to a freak accident at a fairground in July 2003, which she calls "The Great Fall of 2003." Dr. G spent much of that time in and out of the hospital, having many surgeries, and learning how to walk again. Determined not to be stopped in life after everything she went through from a young age, from surviving in the Bronx to being a mother to her two sons, Owen and Joey, she decided she must learn to walk again. And she did. Not only that, but she is now training to go to space and fulfill her dream of seeing Earth, all while inspiring her students to follow their dreams and creating a mirror for others to look at through their windows.

Around the same time as discovering her cockroaches, Dr. G was fascinated with Spider-Man and Peter Parker. She wanted to save the world quietly, just like he did. Then *X-Men* was released, which further sparked her interest in DNA and the mysteries behind the science. Interested in what she was discovering, Dr. G asked the nuns at her school what DNA was and how it happened. Their response proved disappointing for her when they said it was due to God. She craved scientific explanations and was determined to find out more.

In high school, the nuns told her that she would be successful if she graduated and wasn't pregnant. Again, that wasn't good enough for Dr. G. She wanted more than to graduate from school not pregnant. She wanted "to see the Earth with my own eyes. That became my window, while I compared and contrasted how genes behaved."

Despite being told she couldn't go to university because her grades weren't high enough and her mother couldn't afford it, she was determined. And she did! Although everything was against her and she was told it was not possible, she found a way to make it happen and wanted to do well in her first year to prove everyone wrong.

However, at university, she encountered another problem. She was failing her exams despite studying hard for them. She met the man who would later become her rocket scientist husband, and he helped her discover that she learned auditorily rather than visually. After this revelation, her whole college career changed. Four years later, she graduated cum laude with a bachelor of science degree in molecular biology at Rensselaer Polytechnic Institute. Later, she completed a doctoral degree at the California Institute of Technology studying molecular genetics.

Since high school, she has instructed in reading programs, particularly in inner-city areas. "I need to get more people to know that this [science] is an option, not only singing or dancing, not that that's wrong. But I want them to know that even though you come from a non-affluent background, you can still do science—you just have to find the path." As she teaches reading, she also emphasizes its value and importance. Struggling with reading herself, she understands the difficulties some may have with it and how it can be hard not to see a mirror of yourself.

Facing many obstacles over the years to achieve her goal of learning and understanding molecular science, she also faced the discrimination of being a woman and Latina in the STEM field. People have been quick to make assumptions about her journey and have been bold enough to claim to her face that she got to certain places because of her ethnicity rather than her hard work. She explained, "I had comments like, 'You're only here because you're Spanish.' And I'm like, 'No, I earned my spot.' They were devaluing my accomplishments and all the stuff that I earned by saying, 'No, you just got it because of this, not because you earned it,'" Dr. G said in a frustrated, sad tone.

CREATING MIRRORS AND WINDOWS FOR THE YOUNGER GENERATION TO SEE THEMSELVES

Over recent years, the number of females and individuals of color working in STEM has steadily increased, but both groups are still underrepresented in the field.[20] According to the National Science Foundation, although women are equally represented within the college-educated workforce, in science and engineering, women only represent 28 percent of the workforce.[21]

Dr. G asserts that "females and individuals of color are feeling confident enough and know that they deserve the spot at the table and even deserve to lead the table. It should be a collaborative effort. There's no particular face—they're all faces. You see all the mirrors in the windows."

She explained that, over time, mirrors and windows are being created for the younger generation to see themselves in a scientific field. This field looked very different twenty years ago when she entered it or even ten years ago in terms of technology and knowledge. When Dr. G was entering the field, there were no mirrors or windows to look in that reflected someone like her, but now there are, and she is one of them. Thanks to her hard work and determination, others can look up to her as an amazing role model and identify with her, helping them to build their windows for the future.

As I sat with her, her words were an inspiration for me. "Mirrors are inspiring, and windows are for us to really see the

---

[20] "Has the Employment of Women and Minorities in S&E Jobs Increased?" *Stem Education Data*, accessed April 24, 2020.

[21] Ibid.

beauty of other cultures that are similar, yet so different. Let's keep going together."

Despite the statistics showing the slow progress in the number of women and minorities working in STEM, evidence still shows that change must occur. Women are still not as prominent in this field as men. In 2019, two women were due to go on a NASA mission, but only one spacesuit would fit.[22] The mission was delayed for another spacesuit to be made. When Dr. G tried on the smallest unisex size, a medium suit, she still found it to be on the larger side for her small frame. It's surprising—or maybe it isn't—that even NASA isn't quite prepared to have more than one woman go on a mission, or that they don't have well-fitting, female-tailored suits.

To provide some background here, in her early forties after recovering from her fall, Dr. G applied to be a NASA astronaut but received a rejection letter. Determined to still find a way to fulfill her dream of seeing Earth from space, she discovered the PoSSUM Scientist Astronaut Program. As of this writing, if all goes as planned, she will be going to sub-orbit on the *Falcon* in September 2020 with PoSSUM-13[23] to perform microgravity experiments. Her mission will be to "take cloud samples at the mesosphere noctilucent clouds." Along with the pilot and military pilot, she will be doing this a couple of times to collect the samples. She has also applied for the Artemis program for NASA astronauts.

---

22 Mariel Padilla, "First All-Female Spacewalk Is Back On, Nasa Says," The *New York Times*, uploaded October 5, 2019.

23 "Project Possum | The Possum 13," *Project Possum*, accessed May 31, 2020.

Her training to go to space, as you can probably imagine, has been tough and physically demanding. She trains hard every week to be in peak health and looks after her diet, too, which includes a semi-difficult challenge to reduce her Red Bull intake to one a day. Another part of her training is learning technical operations onboard the spacecraft, as well as G-force training at NASA in Florida.

DREAMS CAN COME TRUE IF YOU ENVISION THEM
Many times over the years, Dr. G's dreams did not seem possible. Others told her they would not be possible—whether getting good grades at university or learning how to walk. Dr. G believes "there's no reason for any individual—who is female or is of color—to not be able to find a mirror in this day and age that reflects where they want to be." She stressed that if you have a dream, no matter what it may be, know that you can do it and don't worry about completing it within a certain time.

Her other piece of advice is to take in every moment and make the most of it. Be thankful for the little things. Be thankful for waking up in the morning and having the opportunity to see another day, whatever your day is like. In our society, it can be so easy to think about what we don't have rather than valuing what we do have. The little moments and the little things are too easy to take for granted and not be appreciated.

Sometimes it is not how quickly you get to a certain point, but how you get there. "What's more," Dr. G affirmed, "sometimes those shaky moments were to move you out of something and bring you to something better."

Life may seem confusing or complicated in the moment. I know. I've experienced it. I think we all have at some point. But when you look back at the journey, everything will start to make sense. Everything in Dr. G's journey, my journey, and your journey brought us to where we are now—to this very moment to be reading this line and learning about this incredible woman, who should be a mirror for us all.

LESSONS FROM THIS CHAPTER:
- Believe in yourself.

- You can create your own mirrors, so create them!

- Never give up on your dreams.

- Take every roadblock as a challenge to create something to move forward.

CHAPTER 3

SHERYL SANDBERG IS LEANING IN

Another strong woman who has stepped into a male-dominated field and has more than successfully succeeded is Sheryl Sandberg. Sheryl could arguably be one of the most influential women to mirror, whether you are a high school student, a university student, or an adult. In fact, I am not the only one who shares this opinion. She has been ranked number twelve for *Forbes*'s "America's Self-Made Women 2019," beating Kylie Jenner, fashion mogul Tory Burch, and singer and designer Rihanna.[24] She was also ranked number eighteen on the 2019 *Forbes* "The World's 100 Most Powerful Women" list and is estimated to be worth $1.6 billion.[25]

---

24   "#1415 Sheryl Sandberg," *Forbes*, accessed April 23, 2020.
25   Ibid.

WHO IS THIS AMAZING BILLIONAIRE?

Sheryl is the chief operating officer (COO) at Facebook, a number-one best-selling author of the book *Lean In* and founder of the organization Lean In.

The international organization, cofounded with Rachel Thomas, stems from the idea of her best-selling book and is designed to bring women together to help one another. The mission of the organization is to "help women achieve their ambitions and work to create an equal world."[26] It is designed to help women come together to reach their goals, advocate public policies, and run programs.

As of this writing, the organization has over 40,000 Lean In circles in 170 countries. Anyone can sign up to join a circle, which the website describes as "women who meet regularly to learn new skills, network, and encourage each other."[27]

Other features offered are a newsletter and relevant blog posts about issues surrounding women, such as gender bias. Any gender can join, but it is more tailored toward women, although a section exists specifically for men. Lean In offers many resources to help women uncover various topics from learning about different biases, such as maternal intolerance, to developing leadership skills and learning how to be confident.

Being confident in yourself is key to any type of success. Be confident in your skills and abilities. Be confident in your

---

26 "About the Org," Lean In, accessed April 23 2020.
27 Ibid.

passion and your ability to pursue it. Be confident in your personality and personal value. Confidence doesn't, however, mean being arrogant or cocky but self-assured. It builds over time. Having confidence has taken a while for me. Only when I had been at university for a while did I finally feel like I had it. Growing up, I felt rather unconfident in who I was and in social situations.

This is why university is such an important time. During this time (and high school), we start to learn more about ourselves. The freedom and new experiences challenge us and make us grow, and with this newfound growth comes emerging confidence. When confidence begins to blossom like a tree in spring, so does the feeling of security in ourselves when given the opportunity to try something different, whether that is an activity or going on a weekend trip allowing us to step further out of our comfort zones. At that point, we start to learn more about our dislikes and likes, along with what we feel passionate about. Being passionate about something can be a signal for a potential job or hobby or developing political views.

According to the Lean In website, the organization's goal is to help create "a world where people of every gender can pursue their dreams without bias or other barriers holding them back. Where girls grow up to be confident, resilient leaders. Where more women run companies and countries. We are driven by the belief our society and economy would be better if women and girls were valued as equal to men and boys."[28]

---

28 Ibid.

Bringing a group of hardworking and determined women together to help each other and pick each other up during difficult or challenging times is very powerful—along with learning from one another, building mentors and role models, and creating mirrors to look into.

I experienced the power of working in a group of driven and hardworking women when I spent my junior year working for my university newspaper. By chance, everyone on the staff team, from the editors to the advertising manager, were all women, and being part of it was amazing. I experienced firsthand what it is like to work with strong, young women. Many of the girls have now become inspirations to me and are my mirrors. This has inspired me to work harder and strive for better after learning about how they are stepping into their careers and what they have accomplished at such a young age. I have been lucky enough to experience firsthand how much time and effort goes into producing a weekly university newspaper and how a good team working together can produce something amazing from both work and friendship points of view.

It is no secret that even in our modern-day society, women are still not treated fairly when it comes to gender. Unless we all come together, there will be no change in the world, and gender biases will remain. I love that Sheryl believes so strongly in these messages that she has found a way to share her knowledge and expertise to help better others and let them build mirrors with one another. The Lean In organization has a multitude of free resources available at anyone's fingertips. It is the beginning of making a change for the future.

Networking and connecting with others is critical, particularly in our ever-growing digital world. When we network with others, we are building our mirrors. By meeting new people and exposing ourselves at networking opportunities, we are more likely to grow as we are learning and talking to new individuals. When we step out of comfort zones, we increase our likelihood of finding new role models and mentors to use as mirrors. Even if you dislike networking or feel anxious when the word arises, it is so important to step out and do it! Start by creating a LinkedIn account, if you haven't already done so, and join an organization such as Lean In. Any person you meet in the workplace will always stress the importance of networking, as it helps you grow and learn from others.

WHY DO WE HAVE TOO FEW WOMEN IN THE WORKPLACE?

Over a decade ago in 2010, Sheryl gave a TED Talk called "Why We Have Too Few Women Leaders."[29] She explained why she thinks not many women are in prominent positions within companies. Even though this talk was given a while ago, I still think her advice and lessons are just as important to women as the day she gave them. It is sad to say that, but true.

Her number-one best-selling book, *Lean In*, discusses the topic of her TED Talk in more depth if you want to learn more about it. She also has a book called *Lean In for Graduates*, aimed exclusively at those going into their first job and navigating the workplace for the first time.

---

29 Sheryl Sandberg, "Why We Have Too Few Women Leaders," TED, December 21, 2010, video, 15:28.

In her TED Talk, Sheryl gave some startling statistics about the number of women in politics. She said in the United States, 5 percent of the heads of state were women. She also said that in the United Kingdom, 13 percent of Parliament were women, and in nonprofits, only 20 percent at the top were women.[30]

According to Ranker, as of 2015, in the United States there were seventeen heads of state, which is nearly a 50 percent increase within just five years since her TED Talk, but it still means, overall, only 0.08 percent—not even one full percent—of those heads of state are women.[31] I truly found it shocking how low the percentage is. To me, and I hope to you, women are clearly underrepresented in positions of power despite being in the twenty-first century.

Of course, not every woman is looking to have a position of power in the workforce but rather a good, equal-paying job. Likewise, we do all come from different backgrounds and ethnicities. No journey is the same, and some will find it easier than others to reach the same place. But whatever the goal may be or the background, every woman deserves the opportunity to climb the metaphorical ladder, or as Sheryl likes to describe it, "go through the jungle gym"[32] to reach positions of power. Sheryl also believes every woman should have the opportunity regardless of whether they want or have a family. Having children has been an obstacle that

---

30   Ibid.
31   Mike Rothschild, "Female Presidents Currently in Office," *Ranker*, May 24, 2019.
32   Sheryl Sandberg, "Why We Have Too Few Women Leaders," TED, December 21, 2010, video, 15.28.

typically stopped many females in their career jungle gym as they take the time to look after their families and often put their careers second.

THREE TIPS FROM SHERYL

In her TED Talk,[33] Sheryl covered three tips to help women in the workplace, which are useful for someone at the beginning of her career. By learning from others, such as Sheryl, we can bring that experience and insight into our lives.

TIP NUMBER ONE

"Sit at the Table." She believes women feel intimidated and often stand away from the table during meetings rather than sitting at the table. This is also a metaphor for women not believing in themselves and their ability. "Women systematically underestimate their own abilities," she said. "Men attribute success to themselves; women attribute to external factors."[34]

For me, this raises the question of why women think differently from men. Is it society? Social norms? Perhaps it is not so much the "why" we should focus on, but HOW we can help women think differently, which is what Sheryl is focusing on.

TIP NUMBER TWO

"Make Your Partner a Real Partner." This could be applied to whomever you are living with—a partner or a roommate

---

33 Ibid.
34 Ibid, 5.48-7.03.

or a family member. But whoever it is, be equal in the home responsibilities. Be a team. Organization and forward-thinking with others you surround yourself with will always get you further.[35] Sheryl emphasizes that your partner should be a real partner like you would have in a business. What qualities would you want in a business partner? As a young, unmarried adult, like many others, I don't have to worry about this quite yet, but it is good to know about and keep it in mind when thinking seriously about the future.

TIP NUMBER THREE

"Don't Leave Before You Leave."[36] In her talk, Sheryl recalled a story of a recently graduated student who was already working out what age to have children in terms of her career plan. She wanted to know when she should plan to raise a family even though she wasn't married. "Keep your foot on the gas pedal until the very day you need to leave to take a break for the child, and then make your decisions,"[37] advised Sheryl. It's not necessary to work out when to have children at the beginning of your career. If you want to have a family someday, great, but don't worry about that day until it comes. Never let the idea of wanting a family stop you from reaching for that promotion or climbing through the career jungle gym. Sometimes women feel pressure to work out their family plans at the beginning of their career when they should just focus on their work and figure it out when the time comes.

---

35 Ibid, 9.59-11.30.
36 Ibid, 11.33-12.47.
37 Ibid, 12.52-13.48.

Although two of Sheryl's tips are aimed, for the most part, toward women who are older than the average university graduate, I still think they are important to hear now and even to start thinking about if you are younger or not in the workplace yet. If your goal is to have a career and climb the ladder or navigate the jungle gym, then why not learn from one of the most successful and influential women in the world?

LESSONS FROM THIS CHAPTER:

- Use available resources to learn and develop ideas.

- Understand that women are still vastly unrepresented in positions of leadership.

- Networking leads to meeting new people, who could be mirrors for you.

- Be confident in yourself and let that confidence grow.

- Sit at the table—don't take a backseat to men.

- Make your partner a real partner.

- Don't leave before you leave—plan your career and then decide when it's time to have a family.

CHAPTER 4

BELIEVING IN YOURSELF WITH SUSAN O'DAY

Sheryl Sandberg is the COO at a major corporation. Susan O'Day is the chief information officer (CIO) at one of the most beloved entertainment companies on Earth: the Walt Disney Company.

She may not work directly with Mickey Mouse, but her role is vital within the company and is one not many women have, according to *Fortune 500*. In fact, only 20 percent of CIOs are women.[38] For over a decade, Susan has been the CIO and executive vice president of Enterprise Technology, but she is soon retiring and getting ready to take on new hiking adventures and look after her dogs in sunny Florida.

This isn't the first time Susan has been the CIO of a company. Before her position at Disney, she was CIO and vice president

---

38 Sharon Gillenwater, "2018's State of Women CIOs in the Fortune 500," *Boardroom Insiders*, accessed April 23, 2020.

of Global Shared Services for twelve years at Bristol-Myers Squibb, a global pharmaceutical company. Not only does she have an impressive career, but she is also on the executive board of directors for the 2022 Special Olympics US Games as well as the Alliance for SoCal Innovation Board, a nonprofit organization that directly supports leaders and stakeholders to nurture and grow the SoCal innovation ecosystem.[39]

For the past eight years, Susan has been involved with the Special Olympics, raising over a million dollars in the last few years as well as getting different groups to volunteer. The athletes range from six months to over eighty years old. The volunteers get to meet the athletes and their families, which provides another element to working with this organization and seeing firsthand the impact it has and where the resources go.

I met with Susan in a virtual meeting on our laptops. She sat in her office near the Disney Studios in Burbank, California, as I interviewed her from my bedroom about fifty miles away. It felt surreal to meet the CIO of the Walt Disney Company, and I was nervous. But there was little need to be, as calm and assurance surrounded her. She seemed to be in control. She exuded the poise a person possesses after having been a CIO for over two decades. Her relaxed demeanor assured me this would go well, and it did.

She was wearing glasses, with her blonde shoulder-length hair pulled back while sitting in a white, modern office. I

---

39 "Home – Alliance For Socal Innovation," *Alliance for So Cal Innovation*, accessed May 23. 2020.

imagined this was a very different office than the one she entered when she began her career in technology in the 1980s. Not long after she graduated from St. Lawrence University with a bachelor of art in mathematics, she earned an MBA at the College of William and Mary at t he Mason School of Business before beginning her career.

At the time she started her career, few women were working in technology. Her first job was working at US Railroad on the operations research team helping them understand the math behind laying fiber optics cable for the first time. In this job, Susan realized she liked technology, and from there, she built her career and moved into the field. "I moved into technology because I thought it was more interesting and had more potential. From there, I jumped from doing analysis to operating it, and then I just sort of built a career in tech."

Another aspect of technology Susan liked was that "you can apply it to any discipline." Indeed, it has allowed Susan to have jobs in various areas from working at a railroad company to a pharmaceutical company to an entertainment company. A career in technology has allowed Susan the flexibility to apply it to any industry.

WOMEN IN TECHNOLOGY

Susan has seen more women start working in technology throughout her career. However, she hasn't noticed a significant change in the number of women who are CIOs. Perhaps this is because she has always worked at large corporations, but she found it difficult to recall a time when women represented more than 30 percent of the leaders.

When Susan started working in the 1980s, some women, including Susan, wore bows. Then, when Hillary Rodham Clinton became First Lady and wore a pantsuit, that changed everything for women. "She started wearing pantsuits, and it changed how women literally could dress in the workplace... so it gave a whole bunch of us permission to not have to wear these stupid little bows. You still dressed more masculine than you might have otherwise." Initially, there was an uproar. People could not believe Hillary Clinton's decision, as it was not perceived as "feminine." But the movement inspired other women to start wearing pantsuits, including Susan, who affirmed, "It changed how women could dress in the workplace."

This is just one of the changes Susan has seen in the workplace. When asked why she thinks more women are entering the technology industry, Susan mentioned three reasons, in no particular order. "I think, one, companies have put an emphasis on it. I think, two, there is a bigger pipeline; it's still not huge but it's bigger. At entry level, there is a larger pipeline. And I think, three, women have recognized that it's a field worth working in and that the money is good.... I think those three things have combined to bring more women into tech.... I think that there are more role models obviously to see, and so you're like, 'Oh, she can do that, I can do it, maybe I should go do it.'"

Modern-day women thinking of entering the field of technology now have mirrors of other women to observe, such as Susan. But when Susan and other women from her generation entered this field, they had to build their own windows to look through. When we have role models and can see others who look like us doing something we want to do, it makes the goal and the possibility seem a bit more real. We can learn from them and build personal relationships with our mentors.

DEMAND VERSUS BALANCE

Another potential reason Susan believes fewer women are in the demanding field of technology is that, in general, women, or others who care about having a balance in their lives, are more likely to migrate to asynchronous jobs—jobs that don't require you to be present in real time. For example, a job in which you can talk to someone over e-mail rather than face to face.

Unlike many jobs in the market, core technology jobs appear to be synchronous. They take place in real time and require you to be present to fulfill your job. Susan affirmed, "These core technology jobs are perceived to all be synchronous. They're all real-time, they're all macho, you got to stay 'til midnight, you got to work until your head explodes. If you don't, the world's going to end and everybody relies on it, you know? I think very few jobs are like that, very few. I think if we look at the core technology jobs, engineering jobs, and really look at the structure, there's a way to tease some of them apart to make those jobs more accessible to people who, again, care about having the necessity of a balanced life."

So how does a CIO at Disney with multiple commitments outside of her job keep balance with the different parts of her life? Susan believes it is not one or the other, but it is about integrating. She likes to be clear with herself about her priorities and what is important.

This leads me to reflect on what I consider my top priorities. Do you know yours? What and who does it include? I like this idea because it can be linked to your windows. Priorities are often connected to goals and what you want to achieve. When thinking about your priorities, do you envision anything for the future? For example, one priority is your parents. Why? Because you love them and want to connect with them. Maybe this priority becomes the goal of spending one weekend with them every month to continue building your relationship.

When discussing priorities, Susan shared the story of a woman who works for her and has little children. Between the hours of five to nine in the evening, the woman spends no time on her phone or checking her e-mail. That time is dedicated to being with her children. She values and prioritizes it, wanting to be 100 percent present with them.

After nine, the woman goes back to her phone and e-mails for a few hours to finish up her work. I love this story because this woman knows, prioritizes, and communicates what is important to her with her work peers. She also knows what her goals are and has found a way to both be a mum and have a career.

KNOW YOUR WORTH
"You have to develop confidence in your own worth. I think for women, we often feel like if we're not right there answering the phone really quickly or the e-mail really quickly, they're going to think that I'm not paying attention," Susan said thoughtfully, sitting at her desk.

I have felt like this—whether replying to a text from a friend or responding to an e-mail. If I do not do it quickly, I can easily feel like the other party will think I don't care and am not paying attention. Perhaps it is a natural instinct to want to be liked by others and to think a quick response will help increase the likelihood of this happening. But knowing the two are not correlated and are likely not to have a dramatic impact is important.

If you do feel like this, "Have the confidence to know the world is not going to end if you don't respond within thirty seconds…. I've never had a boss that got irritated if I didn't respond immediately in my whole career," Susan said. Communicate and set expectations with those with whom you work.

Sometimes, in a male-dominated workforce such as technology, it can be easier to think women should adapt to fit in. But that's not the case. Rather, the workforce should be adapting to start mirroring the new environments. Recent statistics show a progression in the number of women having top roles, such as CIOs like Susan. From 2017 to 2018, the number of female CIOs increased by 16 percent.[40] For one year, that is a steep increase, but with women only representing 20 percent of all CIOs, it is fair to say that technology is still a male-dominated industry.

Not only the role of CIO has little female representation; only 5.6 percent of the Fortune 500 CEOs are women, which is

---

40 Sharon Gillenwater, "2018's State of Women CIOs in the Fortune 500," *Boardroom Insiders*, accessed April 23, 2020.

the highest it has ever been at thirty-three companies.[41] I am shocked at how low this statistic is in our modern, post-feminist movement world.

IF YOU KNOW WHAT YOU WANT, DEMAND IT

Susan's advice to anyone, but particularly women, interested in working in technology is to "go deep."

She advises, "Don't be afraid to make sure you get your engineering degree. Go get that core tech and some experience on your resume—some coding, some products you've done so when you are talking to somebody you can show an example of your work. Don't be afraid to get into tech and produce stuff, create stuff. Going into the data field or data analytics, same thing again. I would find ways to work on case studies and practical projects to show an outcome."

"Doing or creating something that has an outcome not only demonstrates your skills and abilities to a potential or current employer but proves it to yourself," Susan said.

She also recommends networking, whether with CIOs, other companies, or your peers. Meeting others and networking is so important, as you never know who might help you land the dream job or help in other ways. Lastly, she recommends being aggressive. More women are needed in technology. "If you know what you want, be demanding, and go for it."

---

41 Claire Zillman, "The Fortune 500 Has More Female CEOs Than Ever Before," *Fortune*, accessed April 23, 2020.

Having a dream job or a high-ranking job didn't cross Susan's mind when she was young. "It never dawned on me in my twenties that I could be the CEO of a company, a big corporate company, and you know, had that dawned on me, I might have done something different in my career, but I don't know."

Perhaps Susan didn't have this realization due to a lack of mirrors when beginning her career. Maybe she didn't realize her potential when looking through her window, as she had limited resources to compare herself to. Have you surrounded yourself with mirrors yet? If you are reading this in high school or university or even in your mid-forties, what do you aspire and dream to do, knowing nothing can limit you?

LESSONS FROM THIS CHAPTER:
- What are your priorities with your time?

- Be confident in your own worth.

- Don't be afraid to go into male-dominated fields if you are female!

- Know your potential.

- Surround yourself with mirrors.

CHAPTER 5

GAY COOK AND LIFE'S SERIES OF EVENTS

———

The last few chapters covered the common theme of networking—a theme in which Gay Cook also strongly believes. If women are finally to break the glass ceiling, they must use networking, along with mirrors and windows, to do so. Gay is a former award-winning newspaper reporter and editor and supporter of women and women's leadership.

When Gay Cook was young, she loved to read and was fascinated by politics. Around this time, she decided to become either a journalist or a lawyer when she grew up. In her junior year of high school, she worked in a law firm doing various assignments. During her senior year, she edited her high school newspaper. Working in a law firm and with her high school newspaper helped decide her career path.

After much contemplation, she decided journalism ultimately would be more interesting than attending law school. She earned a bachelor of science in news-editorial from the

College of Communications at the University of Illinois and later an MA in journalism from the University of Colorado before starting her career.

Fast forward several years later, talking to me on the other side of the phone, Gay said she spent the first half of her career working in the newspaper industry. Over the years, she covered and edited many different stories, enjoying investigative and explanatory journalism most. She has been honored for her work as a reporter and editor at local, state, and national levels.

TELLING THE STORY

Spending most of her journalism career at the *Denver Post*, Gay held different positions both in writing and editing, including being a reporter, editor, editorial page writer, and member of the newspaper's editorial board, ultimately climbing the career ladder to being the paper's managing editor and member of its executive committee.

"I think the hardest part of journalism is maintaining objectivity to the extent that's humanly possible. Telling a story that is compelling and captures and respects the topic and the people about whom you're writing I think are critical. But frankly, you just have to have some guts, because sometimes the stories are very difficult to report on. At the end of the day, it's important to tell the story," Gay remarked seriously and thoughtfully. As she spoke, I imagined a movie reel of stories that she has written and edited flashing through her mind.

Throughout her journalism career, Gay has had many highlights. "It's mixed depending on what you're covering, but there are lots of highlights along the way." One of them was her internship working in Washington, DC, for the late syndicated columnist Jack Anderson, then one of the most highly syndicated columnists in the United States. The following summer she returned to DC, working as a writer for Ralph Nader's Congress Project.

Among the investigative stories she oversaw and edited at the *Denver Post* were those like energy companies taking money from Native Americans by undercutting their oil royalties to an anesthesia manufacturer whose equipment "failed fatal" instead of "failing safe," leading to the deaths of patients in several states. Both projects led to reforms being enacted at the state and federal levels. "Those kind of stories are important to tell and, ultimately, hopefully, made a difference in people's lives," Gay said.

Gay noted that in the last few years, the use of technology and social media has changed the way the public views the world, including how people obtain their news. No longer are newspapers and radio as dominant. When Gay mentioned this, I realized I didn't grow up reading the news much, as I would hear it on the radio and watch the news either at breakfast or dinner. Now, like many others today, I rarely listen to the radio, as I prefer my playlists in the car and around the house. In fact, I didn't notice how little I listen to the radio until I remembered that, as a child, I listened to it on and off throughout the day, either in the car or my bedroom.

Gay was part of the newspaper industry when it was a much more dominant force. She said now "almost anyone can view themselves as a reporter or a journalist without necessarily having the education and credentials that used to be regarded as important to fulfill that role."

After leaving the *Denver Post*, Gay went to work as vice president of executive operations and planning at Metropolitan State College of Denver, now known as the Metropolitan State University of Denver. At that time, it was one of the largest urban baccalaureate colleges in the United States. Today, it continues to have a large and diverse enrollment, with many of its twenty-thousand-plus students being first-generation, meaning they are the first in their families to attend university and earn a degree.[42] This is extremely notable because access to a high-quality affordable education is so essential in the twenty-first century.

Gay then moved to the University of Colorado Anschutz Medical Campus, where she "helped a small team of women doctors and a small advisory board of women leaders" build a Center for Women's Health Research that, since its start, has earned a national reputation for its research into cardiovascular disease, diabetes, and other diseases. When I asked Gay why she jumped from being an award-winning journalist to working in universities, she said it was purely serendipitous.

"Life can be pretty interesting if you're open to engaging in and tackling opportunities that you might never have imagined nor contemplated would come your way. My entree into higher education administration was most serendipitous." It's also true, she added, that one career experience builds to another.

---

42 "About MSU Denver," *MSU Denver*, accessed April 25, 2020.

NETWORK, NETWORK, NETWORK

The large network of people Gay developed as a journalist played a role in every job move she made.

In university, we are often told of the importance of networking and how it can lead to new, unexpected opportunities. Gay advised whatever you do can "expand the range and diversity of the people you know, opening you to new avenues of ideas and ways of thinking, to new opportunities."

A networking connection opened the door to Gay's first internship in DC with syndicated columnist Jack Anderson when she was a college junior. A friend of her father's asked her at a cocktail party about university and what she was planning to do. This friend happened to be closely connected to Jack Anderson and offered to help her secure a summer internship with him. A year later, he helped her land a position on Ralph Nader's Congress Project. "Those two experiences," Gay said, "opened the door to frankly every newspaper job I had."

It is amazing how one choice can lead you down a path. If Gay hadn't gone to the cocktail party, met a friend of her father's, and had a conversation about university, who knows if she would have gone down the same or similar path as she did.

One night when I was a sophomore in university, I felt sick and couldn't sleep. At 3 a.m., I checked my phone and saw an email on LinkedIn from an old friend, asking to connect. I decided then and there, at 3 a.m., to set up my account properly and make it look professional. I know it's random, but what else is there to do in the middle of the night when you're not feeling well in your dorm room that you share? Thanks to that decision, my LinkedIn account has given me two amazing opportunities that are shaping my path. The first is writing this book, and the second is my internship at a digital strategy consultancy. You may not realize it at that moment, but some things open you up to new opportunities to develop your mirrors and windows—just as my LinkedIn account has for me.

Gay strongly believes not only in networking, but also in the importance of a mentor. "Mentors are hugely important. One mentor I had, who is still a good friend, was the first woman in the history of the *Denver Post* to serve on the editorial page and editorial board. Long story very short, she paved the way for me to succeed her on the editorial page when she moved to the business side of the newspaper and mentored me into that role. So I became the second woman editorial writer in the history of the *Denver Post*."

Sometimes we may find mirrors without realizing it, such as in a close friend or a family member. Gay found a mirror in a close friend who not only helped her envision her window of the role she could have one day but helped her make that envisioning a reality.

BREAKING THE GLASS CEILING
Gay is also a past president of the DC-based International Women's Forum (IWF), an organization of more than seven thousand diverse and accomplished women from thirty-three nations on six continents.[43] The IWF has a foundation ded-

---

[43] "About Us Overview," *International Women's Forum*, accessed April 25, 2020.

icated to advancing the next generation of women leaders worldwide. "Mentoring and networking are critical components of the foundation's work to increase the number of women in positions of power and influence," Gay explained, adding that even today, it remains challenging for women to "break the glass ceiling."

Even though women have made marked progress, Gay thinks, and I agree with her, that significant barriers still impede their ability to succeed.

For example, look at the representation of women in the US Congress, where they represent only a quarter of its voting, which unbelievably is a record high in the United States.[44] Yes, more women are in Congress today than in the past, but the percentage remains small. Unequal pay among genders remains a significant problem. And women are still being subjected to sexual harassment in the workplace, which is why the #MeToo movement has become so prominent and powerful in recent years.

"There's much more work to be done in achieving equality than ought to be the case in the twenty-first century," Gay said.

For more than thirty years, women's leadership has been Gay's key focus. In addition to working with the IWF, Gay is a member of the Denver Public Library Friends Foundation, for which she was the president and is now chairing a capital campaign. She believes public libraries across the

---

44   Drew DeSilver. "A record number of women will be serving in the new Congress," *Pew Research Center,* accessed April 25, 2020.

country and the world are "an essential part of a healthy, robust community. I firmly believe that you can't have a great city or town without a great library," she said. Libraries provide access not only to free books but also to resources, programs, and services that enrich people's lives and make communities stronger.

She also just finished board terms on the Latino Community Foundation of Colorado and the Institute for the Advancement of the American Legal System.

YOU FIGURE IT OUT AS YOU GO
Gay is now retired, her last job having been as vice president and corporate officer of the Colorado Trust, a private, philanthropic, grantmaking foundation focused on advancing the health and well-being of the people of Colorado.

In retirement, Gay has had a discovery of a different kind—looking back, she wonders how she ever had time to work. "I know it sounds funny," she said, "but, it's true." When asked how she used to balance her time between work, home, and other commitments, Gay said, "I think you figure it out as you go. Part of it depends on how hard you want to work or how important it is to you. If you're really committed to the work you are doing, and to family life, and having some balance, it's not easy. Things do give along the way, but you figure it out."

"Life is a series of experiences, which is one way to look at it. Just because you might miss one experience along the way because of a choice you've made doesn't mean you won't have an opportunity to engage in it later," she added.

I love what Gay said. It is similar to a saying my family and I often repeat: "Everything happens for a reason."[45] You may not understand what that reason is at the time, but sooner or later, you will find out and it will make sense. Perhaps I am a little fatalistic, but maybe you missed out on one opportunity only to have a better opportunity come along, which, in return, may expand your mirrors and help you move one step closer to your window.

Gay's advice to anyone starting their career is to be persistent. "I would say starting your career is one of the more challenging things most people encounter. Be persistent. Be optimistic and don't give up hope. When you land that first job, learn it and get to understand it. Work hard. And if you find out along the way that's it not for you, it's not the end of the world if you decide to do something different. I think it's important to be open-minded about that. Life is short."

She believes you should be fulfilled and be happy in your career or careers. This isn't stressed often enough in our high school and university system. By having mirrors, we can talk and learn from others about their experiences. We can envision our windows and work out if we think we will be happy pursuing our goals and dreams. And if we think we won't be happy? We can change them. We can change our mirrors, and we can wash our windows to start again. Nothing is permanent. The view through the window isn't set, and that is the beauty of it!

It's reassuring to learn from Gay that starting your career in one field doesn't mean you have to stay in that field. Many

---

45 "A Quote by Marilyn Monroe," Goodreads, accessed April 25, 2020.

younger people struggle to realize this concept. According to a study the Bureau of Labor Statistics conducted, on average, people held 11.7 jobs between the ages of eighteen and forty-eight.[46] I feel it is important for others, regardless of whether you are a student or already working, to learn from Gay's experiences. She started in journalism, moved to higher education administration, helped build a start-up research center on a medical campus, and ended in philanthropy. I know many of my friends and peers feel apprehensive that our majors may not be right for the careers we select. Well, if it turns out not to be, it's okay for us to change, and it happens to many, many people. Remember, Gay said life is short, so why don't we go follow our dreams and goals?

LESSONS FROM THIS CHAPTER:

- Your mirrors and windows may appear unexpectedly—trust the process.

- Mentors can help you on your career path.

- Network, network, network to discover new opportunities.

- Life is short! Go follow your dreams and goals.

- Pursue what you are passionate about.

- Your dreams and goals can shift—follow your passions.

---

46 Jeffrey R. Young, "How Many Times Will People Change Jobs? The Myth of the Endlessly-Job-Hopping Millennial – Edsurge News," *Edsurge,* uploaded July 20, 2017.

CHAPTER 6

ALL YOU NEED IS LOVE AND JACKIE SPENCER TO SHOW YOU THE SIGHTS

Knowing mentors on a personal level isn't the only inspiration we can use to guide us. For instance, the Beatles have inspired many generations of people with ages ranging from five to ninety years old. Their music, lyrics, and stories have captured the hearts of millions across the world. Everyone can name at least one song they like to listen to. I have fond memories of singing "Yellow Submarine" and "Here Comes the Sun" with my family in the car when I was younger. They are one of the few bands that can bring people together, singing along to their songs and enjoying every moment of it.

At the venue where Jackie Spencer's mother and father had their wedding reception, the Beatles were playing upstairs. Jackie was born and raised in Liverpool, and the infamous and much-loved band's music has become the soundtrack to her life.

Jackie has no ordinary nine-to-five job like many of us. She spends her days giving certified Beatles tours around Liverpool in England. It seemingly fits Jackie, as the Beatles have naturally always been part of her life ever since she was a child. "It's funny growing up in Liverpool because you don't necessarily consider yourself a fan because they've always been in my life," she said in her Liverpudlian accent over the phone.

Since the age of sixteen, Jackie has been working in the tourism business. She has owned her Beatles tour business for twenty-five years, meaning this year she is celebrating her silver anniversary. It all started as a fun hobby when she had young children. Now she works full time showing tourists iconic sights around Liverpool and helping them live the Beatles experience for the day.

People from "all over the world, from every walk of life" seek out Jackie's tours. Some have spent years saving up to spend one day touring the city. They've waited for this day to come, full of excitement and wonder. Jackie is known and loved by many for giving them the experience they have always dreamed about and opening their eyes to the magic of the city these once ordinary four boys used to live in. "I think the tours I do are for avid fans who've for their whole life wanted to go to Liverpool and see where their idols grew up."

Like many cities and countries around the world, tourism is key for the city of Liverpool. A report from the Liverpool City Council from 2015 stated, "At the very least, the city needs to maintain standards in its efforts to promote the legacy of the group [the Beatles]. There is a risk to its reputation if it does not attempt to ensure that quality is maintained by all agencies who seek to benefit from facilitating the desire of visitors to explore and access the heritage of the Beatles. At its core, the cultural value of a positive Beatles experience for fans, visitors, and citizens is what underpins the economic impact."[47] The direct impact from Beatles-specific activities is calculated to be £39 million and responsible for 690 jobs in 2014. Therefore, the tourism generated is an essential part of Liverpool's economy.[48]

Before Jackie started her own company, she used to work for the Magical Mystery Tour in Liverpool. There she noticed a gap in the market needed filling. A tour on the Magical Mystery showed coach loads of people around the sights, but she realized the people wanted a more personal one-on-one experience. So in 1995, she took the initiative and created a business of private chauffeur-driven tours to be more personalized, and her business was born. Since then, it has flourished and become her full-time job. Jackie's tours are tailored toward the tourists' wants, and they give a more in-depth experience to Beatles sights, from Penny Lane to Strawberry Fields than you would receive on a coach. In between the sights, Jackie sits in the back of the car with her clients, and together they listen to Beatles music and sing along.

Jackie offers a variety of different upscale tours for people to choose from. According to her website, she has private chauffeur-driven tours, tours with groups, and tours on foot and by bus.[49] Customers can design a tour to visit places they

---

[47] "Beatles Heritage in Liverpool and Its Economics and Its Cultural Sector Impact: a Report for Liverpool City Council," accessed May 24, 2020.

[48] Ibid.

[49] "Tours," *JackieSpencerBeatleGuide*, accessed April 27, 2020.

want to go to specifically. They also have the option to go on a day trip to Wales, where the Beatles spent a lot of their time. And if you think the list ends there, you would be wrong. She even has meet and greets with people who were very close to the Beatles and used to work with them. Her job allows others to achieve their dreams and goals of visiting the city of this iconic band.

Just being a tour guide, however, is not that simple. "It wasn't that I just went out on a bus one day and decided to be a guide. There's a lot more to it than that," she joked. Jackie is a professional, fully trained Blue Badge tour guide. It took her three years to get the certificate. She thinks people have a common misconception about being certified and spending time to earn it. "I am fully qualified, and I've been tested in my knowledge and ability to guide tours."

Over her twenty-five years of touring, she has gained a lot of knowledge around the city, and she loves to learn new things. The most requested spots she is asked to visit are the iconic Penny Lane, Strawberry Fields, John Lennon's bedroom where he dreamed of becoming famous, and the statue on the waterfront. "It's a lovely job because everyone is happy to be here. There's no misery about, and we play music on the way!" she joyfully said.

THE BEATLES AS A WINDOW
When she started her business, she didn't have specific business goals or a window to look through, but she did have the goal of one day making it a full-time job, as she enjoyed giving the tours so much. In 2014, her dream became

reality after quitting her day-to-day government office job. "I don't have a five-year plan. I think it's a good idea not to have a plan. John Lennon said it best: 'Life is what happens while you are busy making plans,'" Jackie said, chuckling over the phone.

But I believe Jackie made her dreams come true by being in the right place and envisioning the Beatles as a way to realize them.

Jackie is acknowledged as being one of the most knowledgeable people on the subject of the Beatles and is recognized as a Beatles expert.[50] Because of this, she has had the opportunity to work with many organizations. In the past, she has worked with Cirque du Soleil, beauty chain Lush, and recently with film crews doing a film on one of the Quarrymen.[51]

Not only is Jackie an expert, but she is a self-proclaimed superfan. "Two years ago, I'll tell you the date exactly, it was the ninth of June 2018. I was standing by a statue of Paul McCartney on Liverpool's waterfront finishing the tour with four people, and the next minute, Paul McCartney got out of a car with James Corden and walked over to pose for pictures. That was without a doubt the best moment," Jackie said, laughing, proclaiming it as the highlight of her career.

---

50   Steve Marinucci, "1958 Liverpool Police Film Believed to Feature Earliest Glimpse of the Beatles," *The Hollywood Reporter,* March 9, 2017.

51   "Tours," *JackieSpencerBeatleGuide,* accessed April 27, 2020.

KEEPING BALANCE

As a self-made, one-woman business minus the tour driver, Jackie does all her own tours, runs her own schedule, and oversees all the other details, including the website and finances. Every year she gives hundreds of tours, some running for as long as two days. Last year, she gave a grand total of 240! That is a tour every day and a half! With a peak season from April to October, her schedule gets extremely busy during the summer. Therefore, winter is a good time for her to recharge and reenergize, spending time with her three children and three grandchildren.

Owning your own business has its pros and cons, said Jackie. She loves being her own boss. She says it's the best part, as you have no one to answer to and can build a schedule that works for you and your lifestyle. The cons, however, are managing all the aspects of the business by yourself if you don't have any help. But this isn't just a business or a source of income for Jackie. "I do it because I love it. I'm kind of really self-sufficient, and I like it that way," she said.

Over the years, Jackie faced challenges before she could run her business as a full-time job—from the decrease in tourism in 2001 due to 9/11 to a major increase in new tour companies flooding the market in 2008, the year Liverpool became the European City of Culture. Being adaptable has allowed her business to grow from strength to strength. This very important quality can be applied to a variety of jobs, especially as the job market is evolving now more than ever thanks to the rapid changes in technology. The more it advances, the more the workplace advances, which will continue for the foreseeable future.

MENTORS AS MIRRORS

Jackie has had three mentors, or mirrors, throughout her life who have impacted her and her business. "These people were the ones who inspired me to do what I'm doing," she said.

Marie Crawford is Jackie's first inspirational mirror. Their friendship and mentorship started when Jackie was full of nerves at the interview to win a place on the Blue Badge Guiding Course. Marie "put me at ease and continues to help me now. She was a tour guide for fifteen years before I started. She also taught Ringo Starr how to read." Now Marie is in her eighties, and she continues to give tours! They have remained friends over the years and often talk with one another.

Her next mirror is Eddie Porter. Jackie met him when she first started working on the Magical Mystery Tour Bus. Eddie was "so generous with his information," teaching her a lot about being a tour guide, which helped shaped her into who she is today.

Jackie's third mirror is her mum. They were at a concert watching a Beatles tribute band when her mum said to her, "You need to go into work tomorrow and give your notice; we'll help you if you struggle, but we don't think you're going to." Thanks to that push, the very next day Jackie walked into her office and handed in her notice at her regular government job to embark on the adventurous world of tour guiding.

Jackie's advice to others is to "do it like I did. Do it as a hobby. Don't give up your regular job at first unless you can afford to or have a fortune in the background. Keep a regular wage coming and do it as a hobby you enjoy. I personally wouldn't give up a good job to start a business. I would do it gradually."

With determination, passion, and love for tour guiding and the Beatles, Jackie created her own window to look through. She surrounded herself with mirrors who guided her, gave advice, and supported her over the years. She learned from the best who had already been in the business and helped her become the success she is today. I like Jackie's story because she never gave up on her goal to be a full-time Beatles guide. Due to her drive and vision, she achieved her goal, and I expect it turned out to be better than she realized it could be.

LESSONS FROM THIS CHAPTER:
- Believe in yourself and your goals.

- Do something that makes you happy and that you love.

- Understand that it is possible to create careers out of hobbies.

- Be adaptable when a hurdle is coming.

- Learn from your mirrors.

CHAPTER 7

SUSAN SANTNER AND THE IMPORTANCE OF BEING HAPPY IN YOUR JOB

Some people, like Jackie Spencer, follow their passion and make their hobby a career. Others go to college hoping to discover their passion. Few people go to university knowing what they want to do when they graduate. However, Susan Santner always knew she wanted to be a nurse.

When Susan was little, her mother was sick, and Susan spent many days in and out of the hospital interacting with the nurses. A few nurses left a lasting impression on her, so much so, she knew she wanted to be a nurse just like them. Their kindness inspired her to choose nursing as a career. From a young age, Susan found a mirror and envisioned a window to look through into the future.

In her last semester at college, Susan did a rotation at LA Children's Hospital. She loved it so much that she found a job as a nurse's aide in a teenage unit. From there, Susan hasn't looked back, spending the past forty-five years working at that very hospital doing a job that she loves. Over the years, her passion hasn't disappeared. It continues to grow and flourish in an environment Susan enjoys working in every day. Now she is the operations manager at Los Angeles Children's Hospital, California. "It's an unusual situation, I think, for people, to get up in the morning and go to work and look forward to it," Susan said.

Susan and I spoke over the phone after one of her weekday shifts had ended. She had a calming quality that made me feel relaxed and at ease as she told me all about her career and job. "It's been a very fulfilling career, and I never dreaded going to work," she reflectively said.

For seven years, Susan was a staff nurse on a general pediatric unit before becoming the operations manager. Now she works with another comanager and four assistant managers to look after a team totaling 140 people. Her responsibilities consist of hiring and retiring employees, budgeting, discipline, and employee engagement.

"In the world of nursing, there are constant changes in practice, medicine, and regulations where you have to be more specific and strict," she said. One change, for example, is the increasing demand for the practice of family nurse practitioners and geriatric specialists in the

United States due to a growing, aging population.[52] As a result, more nurses are choosing to specialize in these particular fields.

According to Susan, her responsibilities and challenges include:

- Communicating with upper management and her staff

- Making sure her nurses are competent and up for providing the safest care

- Keeping the adequate number of staffing per shift when nurses are sick and she doesn't have enough coverage

- Assuring "'my nurses' function as a professional and not a friend with our patients"

This last point is especially difficult for those working in a children's hospital. Working as a nurse in a hospital has many challenges—one of the biggest, perhaps, is knowing that often the patients are very ill and unexpectedly pass away. Creating a balance between being compassionate and caring without getting too close and becoming a friend can be extremely challenging, but it is very important. When the balance between friendship and the patient is lost, it can upset the nurses if something happens to the child unexpectedly. I cannot even begin to imagine such a heartbreak. I have the utmost respect for nurses, doctors, and caregivers who have to deal with these types of situations far more often than we like to think.

---

52 Carson-Newman University Online. "25 Nursing Trends We Expect to See in 2020," *Carson-Newman A Christian University,* uploaded January 6, 2020.

Another challenge is when a nurse who doesn't have a good bedside manner is hired. "When a nurse can't do her job, it's really hard to reteach her," said Susan. Learning the theories and graduating with a degree doesn't necessarily mean someone will be a good nurse. Bedside manner can't be taught. Perhaps the profession of nursing is more art than science.

Regarding what qualities make a good nurse, Susan believes one of the most important characteristics, if not the most important, is having compassion and empathy. "I think if you don't have those two things to reach out and understand what the patient is going through, you're not going to be a good clinician."

One of the best parts of her job, and the reason she wanted to work at a hospital in the first place, is helping others. "It was really about working with people, the challenge of communicating while working with people, trying to grow and help people learn."

Over the years, Susan has had a multitude of feedback that employees want to specifically be on her team. Members of her team report that they are happy and satisfied with their jobs. Susan accomplished her goal of helping her team grow and learn while helping others.

When we use windows to think about our goals and imagine what we want to have one day, we can make a reality. Whether creating a specific environment or team at work or achieving a difficult task, we can be successful when we create windows.

BECOMING A MENTOR FOR OTHERS

Not only is Susan an operational manager, but she is also a part-time instructor working at California State University, West Coast University, and Mount St. Mary's University within the Los Angeles area. "It's for me to teach because I have been a manager for over thirty years. My work is on automatic pilot, and I have very good staff and assistant managers, so I am able to teach as well as work." She has taught a variety of classes over the years, from leadership to being a clinical instructor. When she teaches students at the beginning of their careers, they are very excited and happy, which she said is very gratifying.

I love that Susan not only works with nurses of all ages in the hospital, but also helps with the future generations of nurses and workers by teaching. Her knowledge and wisdom have helped thousands of students get one step closer to achieving their dream jobs. By being their instructor, she has helped many create their window of fulfilling their goals of one day working in the medical profession. Whether she knows it or not, Susan is a mirror to these young nurses.

A FIELD FOR WOMEN

"I think there's more recognition and equality among our administrators, and our doctors, and our nurses than there ever was," Susan asserted. When she first started working at the hospital, there were few women residents. Now she says most of the residents are women.

According to a National Nursing Workforce Study, the number of licensed practitioners/vocational male nurses increased from 7.5 percent in 2015 to 7.8 percent in 2017.[53] This data shows that although the number of male nurses has increased, this field is still very much dominated by female nurses.

However, according to the Association of American Medical Colleges, for the medical profession overall, "Women constitute 50.5 percent of today's medical students, building on steady increases in recent years that saw women account for the majority of first-year students in 2017 and most of the medical school applicants in 2018.[54] Women reached the cusp of the majority in total enrollment last year when they constituted 49.5 percent of all medical students, up from 46.9 percent in 2015.[55]

Although the statistics show that more women are stepping into the medical field, there are still challenges and evidence of it being male-dominated. Susan's daughter's female friend is currently trying to get a residency as a brain surgeon. However, she is finding it difficult, as brain surgeons are typically men. We may be in the year 2020, and a whole new decade, but challenges remain prevalent, and stereotypes still exist and need to be broken.

Susan gives the following advice to her students: "It doesn't matter how much you want to be a nurse, how specialized you want to be, or where you want to work; you have to find

---

[53] "National Nursing Workforce Study, NCSBN," *NCSBN*, accessed April 29, 2020.

[54] Patrick Boyle, "More Women Than Men Are Enrolled in Medical School," *AAMC*, accessed April 29, 2020.

[55] Ibid.

a good leader. If the leader isn't good, the staff won't be happy and you won't be happy."

Good leaders understand what it is like to be in the place of those they are managing. Good leadership decisions are best made when leaders understand the groundwork and build their careers to become leaders. Leaders become mentors and mirrors. When we can find someone to guide us, like Susan, to show us examples of who we can become, we become stronger and more specific when building our windows.

When I think of strong leadership, I think of the national club Her Campus, which I am part of at my university. The leadership from the students on the executive team has taught me the importance of communication among chapter members, how empowering it can be to make a team strong and happy, and how to support others in times of need. Watching these girls and their leadership has allowed me to learn important skills and valuable lessons. Each, in different ways, has been a mirror for me.

KEEP A BALANCE
If Susan could have done anything differently, she wishes she had earned her bachelor's degree earlier at the beginning of her career. Other than that, she has loved everything about her career and her job. But she advises keeping a balance in your life with work and home. "Do something that is enriching and fun to forget about work," she thoughtfully said on the phone.

We all should take this important piece of advice. Sometimes it is so easy to revolve 99 percent of our lives around work and stress. We need to leave enough time to do something we enjoy. Susan always recommends her nurses have a stable home life and outside activities. In fact, at her hospital, the nurses are offered a variety of activities, such as exercise and mindfulness, which has been proven to help their stress and anxiety.

Mindfulness can help nurses increase their compassion and empathy with patients.[56] Working in an environment that has an intense focus on these abilities can be draining and actually lead to a deficit of these qualities when interacting with patients. Practicing meditation can strengthen responsiveness to compassion and leave the nurse feeling happier overall.[57]

In general, not enough emphasis is placed on mindfulness and looking after our mental health. Many jobs and working environments, such as nursing, create a lot of stress in day-to-day life. When we don't deal with our stress in an effective way, it builds up inside of us. As a result, some will get a migraine, others will have an irritable bowel syndrome (IBS) attack, or some may unleash their stress verbally on those close to them. I love that Susan's hospital recognizes the importance of mindfulness and are utilizing it in a practical way to help workers.

With a three-year nursing degree, a person can make $75,000 in the first year. Nursing is a popular career that many are choosing. To keep that necessary balance, Susan offers an alternative thought. "Working three days a week, many nurses

---

56   Sandra Bernstein, "Being Present," *Nursing* 49, no. 6 (June 2019): 14-17.
57   Ibid.

spend the rest of their week traveling and exploring, some even as far as a long weekend away in Paris. Although it may not be the highest-paying job," Susan advised, "you can make a nice living and still have wonderful time off to re-enrich yourself." Being flexible appeals to many and perhaps explains its popularity in particular with women, as they have more flexibility to raise a family.

Susan finally noted, "The greatest challenge is making a decision when you're eighteen or nineteen years old about how to spend your life when you haven't really lived your life enough to really know. Maybe work for a year or two before starting college. These are very big decisions for young people. Young people today have high expectations. I think you should have high expectations, and I think you should have dreams. You should be excited because that is what will make you successful. Be engaged and excited, and you'll be fine."

LESSONS FROM THIS CHAPTER:

- Mirrors can lead you to passion.

- Help others achieve their windows when possible.

- Find a job that makes you happy to get out of bed in the morning.

CHAPTER 8

BUILDING HUNDREDS OF MIRRORS WITH DEBRA BENTON

―

Some people like Susan Santner know what type of career they want and spend their whole lives working in it. Debra Benton, however, has a different story. Debra spent the first few years of her career working as one of fifteen women at a special management trainee program at a computer company, but not all went as planned. A few years into the job, Debra's boss decided to let her go. He thought that Debra didn't get on well with the men...and it caused issues.

At the age of twenty-three, in 1976, Debra started her own executive coaching business. After being turned away from her job, she took matters into her own hands and decided to go on an outplacement process to help evaluate her strengths and weaknesses. She also spent time researching how to get along well with men! Putting together all the information she had gathered during her research and the knowledge she had accumulated allowed her to start her business. Since the day it started, her business has thrived, and she has helped many individuals, mainly male executives, learn how to get along better with those in the workplace. She specializes in leadership mentoring, succession planning, and CEO presence.[58]

Debra has helped people, from managers to executives, develop their leadership skills. Having spent numerous years working in this field, she is considered an expert. She has been featured on many front pages of publications like the *Wall Street Journal* and *USA Today,* and she has also been the welcome guest on the *Today Show, Good Morning America*, and CNN. These are just the beginnings of her accomplishments. She has also published eleven books that have been translated into a dozen different languages. When she isn't working with individuals, she is teaching leadership in Colorado State University's MBA Global Social & Sustainable Enterprise program and is an adjunct professor at the University of Northern Colorado Monfort School of Business.

Debra has been ranked one of the top ten executive coaches in the world and the number-one female coach in 2013.[59] When I asked her on a phone call what differentiates her work from others', she said she thinks it must be that she is a one-person operation. She spends her time with individuals one-on-one giving advice tailored to them.

---

58 "Debra Benton – Words for the Whole of Your Career," *Debra Benton,* accessed April 30, 2020.

59 Ibid.

THE IMPORTANCE OF A MIRROR

Over the years, Debra has worked with and coached many accomplished people who are widely recognized around the world, from lawyer Amal Clooney to composer Lin Manuel Miranda. She enjoys the process of helping others by coaching them to become even better at what they do.

The mirrors she surrounded herself with helped Debra build the career she has today. Over the years, she has accumulated many different mirrors from all corners of the world, helping her grow her business, advising her, and creating her windows to look through.

"I've had great exposure over the years to wonderful mentors from around the world; I've had easily one hundred people I would call mentors. They've helped us along the way with how to handle situations, how to do well, how to be better in every aspect of my career. I'm able to help others with that information. I just have a wonderful library of advice from the streets, not from theory...from somebody who has actually been there, done that, and they saw fit to help me," Debra remarked.

Having mentors and someone to guide you along the way is so important. We know we can navigate paths by ourselves, but having someone with us helps the process and the decisions we make along the way. When I started university, I was given a peer mentor. Lost and relatively scared starting a new chapter by myself, I had so many questions about how simple things worked that no one told me about. However, I could turn to my peer mentor. She helped guide me in many directions, answered my questions, and encouraged me to join some clubs on campus that she joined when she was a freshman, one of them being Her Campus. Without her mentoring, I would have remained lost and probably would not have been guided to where I am today.

"Having a mentor is like having good parents," Debra said. "Someone who starts you out right in life, like a mentor, someone who is outside of your family, so to speak, like a teacher or a coach. It's very important to have people who have been through the situations you are going to go through and teach you what they've learned. It doesn't mean you have to do what they've done, because you need to learn from your own mistakes and own experiences," Debra advised.

Debra believes in the importance and usefulness of having mirrors in your life. "It is useful to have more than one mentor in your career," Debra asserted. She believes you should have one in each area of your life, whether for finances or how to market your business. "When you are younger, you look up to older people for mentors. When you are older, you look to younger people to be your mentors," she said, "but you can learn from both. It's very much reciprocal, and there's so much to be learned from the younger generation."

Both sides are "meeting different types of people, understanding different experiences, and really growing their own network of young, up-and-coming professionals to be able to support or to be able to offer opportunities," said Jenni Luke, chief executive of national teen mentoring organization Step Up, in a *New York Times* article.[60]

---

60 Lizz Schumer, "Why Mentoring Matters, and How to Get Started," *New York Times*, uploaded September 26, 2018.

This idea of having senior-youth mentorships is practiced in many senior living spaces. According to a Sunrise Senior Living article, people of younger generations, from elementary students to young adults, are being paired with a senior living at its facilities. This program has many benefits, such as breaking ageism, bridging the generation gap, and giving purpose to lonely seniors who rarely see family. The "mentoring benefits older adults as much as it does the younger generation being mentored."[61] Both sides can learn so much from one another as well as develop companionship.

"Like I said earlier, I have worked with over one hundred CEOs who have taken me under their wings and wanted to teach me what they know and help me become better," Debra reflected. "It's a wealth of experience that you cannot get from a book, from school, or from a job."

A 2015 study from the University of California Haas School of Business found that "women gained more social capital from affiliation with a high-status mentor than their male counterparts did, according to a *New York Times* article, which also reported that the Department of Labor indicated 57 percent of women participate in the workforce." Therefore, having mentorships may be more valuable than many realize.[62]

Mentors should be "someone you establish a friendship with. Stay in touch. Ask for their help or their advice or their experience, and then follow up and tell them what their advice

---

[61] "Senior Mentors: How to Connect with a Mentoring Project That Makes a Difference," *Sunrise Senior Living*, accessed May 26, 2020.

[62] Lizz Schumer, "Why Mentoring Matters, and How to Get Started," *New York Times*, uploaded September 26, 2018.

or opinion or experience helped you do. And then they'll want to help you again. You want that kind of relationship," advised Debra.

I consider some friends who are a year ahead of me at university to be mentors. When I had to decide which university to attend, I messaged some of them. We had a long chat and I asked about their experiences and for their advice. I had the choice to live at home and commute to class daily or live on campus about an hour from home. The choice was tough for me, and I spent days agonizing over the decision. Without their help and listening to their stories, I would not have made my choice so confidently to move away from home. Throughout university, I have been lucky enough to get advice from them, and they pushed me to have new adventures. Having a relationship—even better, having a friendship—with a mentor is a lovely bond to build. Not only does it connect you both in a richer way, but you can also be there for one another.

BE HANDS-ON

To understand and learn in the best way, Debra thinks mentorship should be hands-on. Gaining experience rather than learning about it in a textbook or in school is more valuable and useful. "I have often said it would be wonderful if when a person gets out of education and they start their career, they could work directly for a really good CEO. Then work up from ground level. Working for both good and bad CEOs, you will learn," said Debra.

I agree with Debra. Students often spend far too much time learning about theories and figures for a test when the best lessons come from experiencing and doing something hands-on in the real world. You can learn about communication and the psychology behind relationships until you become an expert, but it will not help you communicate in relationships until you practice it. As a communications major, I have spent a lot of time studying social media and theories behind the interaction, but only during my internship did I understand how to engage with strangers and build followers.

When Debra started her career, the people sent to her were mainly white men (ironic considering she lost her other job because she had bad relationships with men). Then for about ten years after, black men were sent to her for coaching. Now, in the last fifteen years or so, women are being sent to her. Men of various ethnic backgrounds are still sent to her, but the increase in the number of women has been noticeable. Both genders are just as capable of having leadership roles, and both have different advantages. Of course, these patterns follow major movements in the United States from the Civil Rights Movement to Female Empowerment, which is likely why her client demographic changed. "Whatever the gender may be, a good leader is a good leader," Debra admitted.

I agree with Debra that a good leader is a good leader regardless of gender, but now more female leaders are coming into upper-level positions. Remember Chapter 4 with Susan O'Day? More women are slowly obtaining CIO and CEO roles! Statistics show that more women are becoming leaders, which is great news even if it is slow and far too many years too late.

THE WORKPLACE IS CHANGING

"Learn from a coach, a boss, or a mentor what you did not learn at home," Debra said. There are many ways to learn good skills and develop your thinking as adults. "Having a good foundation at a young age is always helpful, but if not, then there are other ways to build skills and foundations for your career," she said.

The best way to grow as an individual is to step outside your comfort zone and embrace the changes. To do this, Debra suggested taking baby steps. For example, if you want to introduce yourself to the CEO, nothing is stopping you from doing so. Make a point to go up and say something. "Do something you wouldn't normally, something that makes you uncomfortable, because you never know what will come out of it." Remain consistent at making baby steps to continue to grow. Stepping outside your comfort zone gives you new opportunities. Those new opportunities can be new mirrors that can open up yours.

In her new book, *The Leadership Mind Switch: Rethinking How We Think in the New World of Work,* Debra explores the new world of work. With the changes in technology, politics, and a growing diverse population, the work world is rapidly evolving from where it used to be. "My generation is probably the last where there was an American dream and a certain kind of family structure, and a certain type of honesty and integrity that was the norm. With a growing diverse audience and expectations, perceptions are changing along with definitions. I may see one situation differently from how you may see it. It was simpler in the early days," Debra said.

WHAT MAKES YOU DIFFERENT?

Debra's advice to university-aged students is: "Don't rely on learning what everybody else is learning." While teaching a university class, she asked her students questions. She first asked them to raise their hands if they had a pretty good GPA. Everybody in the room raised their hands. She then asked if they have had a pretty good university experience and good extracurricular activities. All the students raised their hands again. The last question was how many of them were ambitious and ready to conquer the world? Again, they all raised their hands. Then, she questioned, "Now how is anybody going to be able to distinguish you from anybody else if you're all doing the same thing?"

Choosing other sources to learn from distinguishes you from your peers. You want to stand out enough to future employers and differentiate yourself from peers in the same position. Debra noted that having a positive viewpoint will separate you from those who have a negative aspect about them.

Debra also suggests, "If your career goal is to climb the ladder higher and higher, you want to reach those who are already at that higher level." Years ago, she was quoted in *Savvy* magazine: "Amateurs teach amateurs how to be amateur." At the time, she got a lot of flak for it, but she strongly believed in it. "If you want to learn how to be the best, you need to learn from the best, even if you cannot personally be around that person you aspire to be." With access to LinkedIn, online articles, YouTube, and much more, you can learn about that person and let them mentor you even if they do not know you personally.

WHAT DEBRA WISHES...

If Debra could restart her career again, she wishes that she had followed her own advice of being more courageous, even though she was already fearless at starting her own business at the age of twenty-three. In addition, when she was younger, a man once admired her courage and told her, "What I like about you is you do what most women won't in terms of having the courage to ask for more money or expecting to be given a seat at the table."

She also wishes she had stayed in better contact with the people she met early on in her career. "At the beginning, you still have another thirty or forty years until retirement. When you meet other young people, they too still have around the same number of years left in their careers. You never know who they will become in their years later." This is a great lesson to learn now if you are a high school student, university student, or still at the beginning of your career.

Debra's final advice to me left a great impression. "Understand what makes you up as a person." It could be family, work, health and exercise, sport, hobbies, politics, art, piano, hugging your dog—the list goes on. Balancing our time can be difficult and frustrating. Debra's advice to her clients and to me was, "Spend at least four minutes every day doing a little of something you love. Sometimes it will multiply to fourteen minutes or forty minutes, but don't lose something that's important to you, because none of us have enough time."

LESSONS FROM THIS CHAPTER:

- Careers can evolve.

- Have as many mentors as you can so you can learn from a variety of people!

- Build relationships with your mentors. Even better, develop a friendship with them.

- Get experience and be hands-on.

- Figure out what makes you different from the crowd and use it.

CHAPTER 9

JUDITH HEUMANN'S FIGHT FOR CHANGE

Debra changes people's lives by coaching them and helping them be better leaders. She has changed the world of many CEOs and teams by helping them communicate more efficiently with one another. Judith Heumann changes people's lives by being one of the main people behind the disability rights movement in the United States.

I sat captivated as I watched Judith in the middle of the stage in her wheelchair cracking jokes, making the whole TED Talk[63] audience laugh, including myself on the other side of my laptop screen. She shared her life story with the audience and recalled some of its pivotal moments along with how her voice has changed, quite literally, the world.

---

63 Judith Heumann, "Our Fight for Disability Rights - And Why We're Not Done Yet," TEDxMidAtlantic, March 2018, Video, 17.02.

If you haven't heard of Judith Heumann, I'll catch you up now. She is a world-renowned disability rights activist who is the catalyst behind much of the disability rights movement in the United States. From a young age, Judith was determined to make a change for others after facing discrimination for her disability.

She has worked for both the Obama and Clinton administrations and the State Department. Judith has received many awards over the years, along with six honorary doctorates. She earned a master's in public health at the University of California, Berkeley. Over forty years ago, she helped lead a protest called the 504 Sit-In. Disability rights activists occupied a federal building for almost a month and demanded greater accessibility.[64]

JUDITH'S STORY

When Judith was eighteen months old, she contracted polio and has been bound to a wheelchair ever since. When she was a child, she was not allowed to attend public school, as her wheelchair was determined a fire hazard. Instead, a teacher was sent to her house for two-and-a-half hours a week. When she was nine years old, she finally went to school for the first time with other students, but it wasn't a regular school. It was a place where disabled students went, and the ages ranged all the way to twenty-one years old.

Her parents were German Jews who escaped the Holocaust. Together, they were determined to make a change for their

---

64 Andrew Grim, "Sitting-In for Disability Rights: The Section 504 Protests of the 1970s," *National Museum of American History*, uploaded July 8, 2015.

child to go to a regular high school and have normal classes, which would allow her to have an appropriate education. Working with other parents facing similar situations with their children, they rounded up and went to the Board of Education to demand a change in accessibility in high schools. The board took action, and, finally, Judith and other students like her could go to a regular high school and take normal classes.

After high school, Judith went to Long Island University to study to be a teacher. She took all the required courses to be prepared for the license exams she had to take after university to qualify. When her exams arrived, her friends carried her up the stairs of the building where they were taking place. She passed both the oral and written portions of the test. However, she did not pass the medical exam and was denied her teacher's certificate because she couldn't walk. She then discovered no disabled teachers used wheelchairs.

Through her experiences with the education system, Judith learned a valuable lesson. "I was learning more and more what discrimination was, and, equally important, I was learning that I needed to become my own advocate.[65]

FIGHTING THE EDUCATION SYSTEM…AGAIN

This was the first time she challenged the system, following the footsteps of her parents. She spoke to a friend who had a friend connected to the *New York Times*. They connected Judith to a reporter to write a piece about what was happening.

---

65   Judith Heumann, "Our Fight for Disability Rights - And Why We're Not Done Yet," TEDxMidAtlantic, March 2018, Video, 17.02, (4.08-4.55).

The next day, an editorial appeared in the *Times* titled, "Heumann v. The Board of Education."[66]

The same day the article came out, Judith received a call from an attorney who was writing a book on civil rights. He wanted to interview her about the article. At the end of the interview, Judith asked the attorney to represent her, as she wanted to sue the Board of Education. He agreed, and the case was taken to court.

Judith believes what happened next was nothing less than the stars aligning. The first female African American judge, Constance Baker Motley, was assigned to her court case. Judge Motley ordered the Board of Education to give Judith another medical exam. The board did, and Judith got her teaching certificate. It was a huge moment for her. It was the first time she'd challenged the system, and it resulted in her making a change and getting the dream she'd always wanted. Judith returned to the same school she attended in second grade and taught there.

Just like Judith, I, too, think all the stars were aligned for her to get to this point of winning the court case. She was meant to make this difference in the world. Without her parents being strong and determined to demand their daughter and others the right to go to a regular high school and the Board of Education allowing it, Judith probably would not have been led to this moment. Because of the newspaper article, the interview, and the judge, it was meant to be. I quoted

---

[66] Andrew H Malcom, "Woman in Wheelchair Sues to Become Teacher," *New York Times,* May 27, 1970.

earlier in the book, "Everything happens for a reason," from Marilyn Monroe,[67] and I believe it now more than ever after learning from these inspiring stories.

Judith's goal was to get her teaching license and not be discriminated against for using a wheelchair to move around. She used her window to envision what she wanted to happen, and she was looking through it the whole time, never shutting the blinds or looking away. At the beginning of her court case, she was not entirely sure how it would end, but she knew the result she desired and believed it would happen, and it did! That is the power of having goals and using windows. When you can see it, feel it, and imagine it, it will likely happen.

LOOKING THROUGH MORE WINDOWS AND SEEING CHANGE

Judith and her friends realized they needed to work together to make even further changes. Both the Civil Rights and Women's Rights Movements occurred at the time. "We were learning from them about their activism and their ability to come together, not only to discuss problems but to discuss solutions. And from this was born what we call today the Disability Rights Movement,"[68] Judith said.

In her TED Talk, Judith explained that in 1972, President Richard Nixon vetoed the Rehabilitation Act. She and her group protested. When the regulations to implement the

---

67   "A Quote by Marilyn Monroe," Goodreads, accessed April 25, 2020.
68   Judith Heumann, "Our Fight for Disability Rights – And Why We're Not Done Yet," TEDxMidAtlantic, March 2018, Video, 17.02, (8.49-9.30).

bill into law had to be signed, Judith's group demonstrated again. Despite their demonstrations, Nixon went ahead and signed. It then seemed the Americans with Disabilities Act (ADA) might not be signed. "So," Judith said, "the disabled people from all across the United States came together and crawled up the Capitol steps."[69] With a smile on her face, she recalled it being an amazing day, which resulted in the ADA being signed by the House and Senate. President George H. W. Bush then signed it in front of the White House on the lawn with two thousand people. In his speech, President Bush made this famous statement: "Let the shameful walls of exclusion finally come tumbling down."[70]

This year, *TIME Magazine* is running a project called "100 Women of the Year." For seventy-two years, they have been naming "Man of the Year" until it changed in 1999 to "Person of the Year." That means there are seventy-two years' worth of unrecognized women of the year! *TIME Magazine*'s project is "spotlighting influential women who were often overshadowed."[71] For the year 1977, Judith has been recognized as Women of the Year for her work during the 504 Sit-In.

Not long ago, being a disabled person meant having limited access in the world. There weren't ramps to get on public transportation, accessible bathrooms in the mall, nor Braille or a sign language interpreter. As a member of Generation Z, I cannot imagine a world without accessibility, as I have

---

69   Ibid, 10.46-12.08.

70   Ibid, 10.46-12.08.

71   "Judith Heumann 100 Women of the Year." *TIME Magazine*. Uploaded March 5, 2020.

always seen it in action. Having no accessible bathrooms or ramps for wheelchairs seems so alien and unbelievable to me. Thankfully, life in the United States has changed. According to Judith, "These things have changed, and they have inspired the world. Disabled people around the world want the laws we have, and they want those laws enforced."[72]

WE'RE IN THIS TOGETHER

Judith ended her TED Talk with a very powerful quote that touched me. It applies not only to disability discrimination, but also to any injustice. "Together we can make a difference. Together we can speak up for justice. Together we can change the world."[73] Judith is one of my mirrors. Her inspiration, determination, and drive amaze me as I learn about what she has done in the world and how she's helped others.

As a white, nondisabled young woman who leads a privileged life compared to most, I cannot compare my life or understand the degrees of discrimination Judith has faced. But I admire the significant work she has done to change the world.

When I moved to Los Angeles, I was shocked at the amount of racial discrimination still present in the culture. I was born and raised in a predominately white, middle-class area, so moving to one of the world's most diverse cities was a major eye-opener for me. I knew, of course, that discrimination issues still existed, but I did not know to what extent. Whether the discrimination is based on race, gender bias, sexuality

---

72   Ibid.
73   Ibid.

preference, disability, or even age, our society still has a lot of room for change.

When I moved here, I was shocked to see that everyone had either Mexican or Latino gardeners and cleaners. The average person in England doesn't have this type of help. To have the gardener come round was considered a treat or necessary for a major job. But the treatment of the workers surprised me more. I watch people ignore them while they worked on their properties. I learned about racial slurs and overheard mean conversations. It shocked me that so many still looked at others with this mindset.

Just like Judith Heumann, other women have changed the world. Dr. Elizabeth Blackwell was the first woman to receive a medical degree from an American medical school in the mid-1800s.[74] She went to an all-male institution. Thanks to her determination and bravery, other women soon followed in her footsteps and earned medical degrees. In more recent years, Ellen Johnson-Sirleaf was the first elected woman head of state in Africa.[75] In 2006, she became the president of Liberia. When she went into office, she created significant change for the better of the country and its people, such as fighting poverty for women and girls. President Sirleaf had such an outstanding impact that, in 2011, she awarded the Nobel Peace Prize for her "nonviolent role in promoting peace, democracy, and gender equality" when working with two other female leaders, Leymah Gbowee and Tawakkol Karman.[76]

---

74 One, "12 Women Who Changed The World," uploaded March 6, 2020.

75 Ibid.

76 Ibid.

"Together we can make a difference," Judith said at the end of her TED Talk.[77] If we use Judith or one of the other women mentioned above like a mirror, we can create change. We can make it happen together. If we follow in these women's footsteps and gather the courage that they had, we, too, can look through our windows with the same kind of eyes. We must envision the change happening, whether it is a little change or a big change. If we see the need for a change regarding discrimination, each one of us can make a difference, just as Judith has.

LESSONS FROM THIS CHAPTER:

- Anything is possible. Use your mirrors and believe!

- Don't lose focus when looking through your windows.

- Stand up for what you believe in to help others.

- Don't settle for any type of injustice.

- Together we can make a difference.

---

77 Judith Heumann, "Our Fight for Disability Rights - And Why We're Not Done Yet," TEDxMidAtlantic, March 2018, Video, 17.02, (16.31-16.47).

CHAPTER 10

VISUALIZATION AND ITS POWER

Judith Heumann is changing lives through law and accessibility, and Ashanti Johnson is changing lives by helping others feel strong and happy within their own bodies. Ashanti had no specific plan, only a visualization and a dream. With those two things, she decided one day to resign from her job and take a leap to what would become a successful physical and mental fitness company. Since the start of her company, 360.Mind.Body.Soul, in 2010, she has helped hundreds lose thousands of pounds.

Ashanti opened her 2018 TED Talk, "The Power of Visualization," by describing her average morning in 2009.[78] Every day, she would sit on her balcony with her coffee and look down at the parking lot below her. But instead of seeing the parking lot, she imagined that one day it would be her fitness gym parking lot.

---

78   Ashanti Johnson, "The Power of Visualization, TEDxWillowCreek," YouTube, May 16, 2018, Video, 15:43.

After some thought, with no specific plan or funds, Ashanti decided to resign from her job. The next Monday, she taught her first boot camp lesson on the beach for sixteen ladies. During the following year, every morning, she visualized her boot camp and fitness business and dreamed of everything she wanted to have one day. Over time, her visions started to intensify due to her "taking the steps toward the vision. Every vision would just unfold a little bit more, and it was becoming real."[79]

She taught her boot camp on the beach every day for five months until winter came and it became too cold. She then decided to look for a place to sublease. After three weeks, she eventually found a potential place, but the town had been nicknamed Terror Town. Unsure what to do, she decided to check out the place and follow her vision. Little did she know that she would fall in love with the building. Inside was a quirky converted art gallery that had eighteen-foot-high ceilings and decorated doors.

Everything about the place felt right to Ashanti, and she knew she needed to start her gym here. Then the subleaser, a petite woman, asked how much she could afford instead of telling her how much it was. After replying $400, Ashanti and the woman agreed, and the deal was sealed.

"I got on my grind [you guys] for a year; I was a one-woman force. I taught every single class on the schedule, over thirty classes a week. I mopped the floors. I answered the phones. I did all the marketing, created posters,"[80] Ashanti said. She

---

79 Ibid, 1.45-1.55.

80 Ibid, 5.34-6.00.

worked hard to do everything that came with starting her business, and in the second year, she created a team to help her. Her boot camp went from sixteen to over 150 people in just over a year.

"One day, I'm driving to the gym, I pull into the parking lot, and I'm faced with an undeniable sight. That parking lot looked just like the one I envisioned all those years on my balcony. That vision became reality,"[81] Ashanti affirmed. After years of imagining something, she realized it was now her reality. She was literally sitting in the middle of her vision.

THE BENEFITS OF VISUALIZATION

Ashanti explained that one benefit of visualization is that it helps you clarify what you want. "It's not the act of creation because you already know what you want. You just may not have created the space to allow it to come up."[82] This is what she was doing on her balcony a decade ago when her vision of the gym developed. While she stood on her balcony, she clarified what her vision was along with the energy she placed around it. Sometimes, negative energy can appear with the visualization, but do not panic. You just need to allow yourself to root that out.

Ashanti explained that negative energy often appears when people want to lose weight. Once they've worked out their goal weight or how much they need to lose, it can suddenly become negative rather than positive. Losing weight can seem like a goal

---

[81] Ibid, 6.56-7.14.

[82] Ibid, 8.09-8.16.

that is too far to reach. Her clients often think of every reason why they won't reach their weight goals. But these thoughts and negative energy become an opportunity to practice mental fitness to reach their goal, which is the second benefit.

THE VISUALIZATION PROCESS

In the next part of her talk, Ashanti walked the audience through a visualizing process that she says should be practiced often to help you reach your goals.

- First, quiet your mind as much as possible. Imagine yourself in a safe, comforting place you like to be in. Bring as much detail to the vision as you can, from how the surface feels underneath you where you are sitting to the air surrounding you. She says that quieting your mind has been proven to help visualization.

- Then pick an area in your life to visualize a manifestation happening in that moment. It can be physical such as losing weight or gaining muscle or healing an injury. Or choose a conflict in your life, like mending an argument with a family member or working on yourself to stop procrastinating. Likewise, you could also pick a goal you want to accomplish. It can be one you have started or one you would like to start.

- Then work out the energy around it. Is it positive or negative? If it is negative, root it out.

- Once you've completed the visualization and felt the experience, slowly bring yourself back to reality.

"You are a creator. Creators must create. This visualization will help you determine what you want, and then the mental fitness will help you to root out any negativity so that you can fully realize your vision,"[83] Ashanti advised.

MY OWN RESULTING VISUALIZATION

At this point in her TED Talk, I realized I had previously practiced visualization like Ashanti did. When I was a child, I used to get very nervous about doing short presentations in front of my class. My mum always told me to imagine the audience sitting on the toilet. Now, imagining your peers sitting on the toilet is not my favorite image to have in my head, but it did make a difference to six-year-old Rosie. I realized that everyone in that room is human, just like me. They weren't scary, nor should I be scared to do that presentation. I didn't realize back then that I was practicing the power of visualization. It turns out I have been practicing it for a long time, and I suspect you have, too.

She commented to her audience, "Imagine what you could accomplish if you put some intentions into your vision. I think it is a shame that school and university students are not taught the importance of mindfulness and about how powerful our brains are."

When I struggled to ride my bike for the first time with two wheels instead of four, my grandfather told me to imagine riding across the playing field all by myself. Every wobble, every scraped knee, and every time I put my feet down to

---

83   Ibid, 15.14-15.32.

stop myself from falling off, I was reminded to imagine what it would be like to finally ride on two wheels all by myself. I was thinking of the bigger picture. I imagined all the places I could go when I got a little older; I could ride around the park and go pick up a snack at the local shop all by myself. But to do this, I needed to teach myself to ride my bike and to trust it and myself. I can't remember exactly how long or how many hours of practice it took, but I do know I did it. With some encouragement from my grandfather and a little visualization, I eventually managed to ride all by myself on two wheels. This pastime has continued to be one of my favorite activities.

I could list all the times I have unknowingly practiced visualization throughout my short twenty-plus years of life, but that would bore you pretty quickly. I'm sure you, too, have examples where you have unconsciously practiced it. Do you remember how that visualization made you feel? Whenever I have visualized anything, it helped it feel more real and possible. Sometimes, when we are faced with a challenge or something that seems out of reach, it can feel impossible to do. But practicing visualization can help it feel possible and achievable. By practicing visualization, you also tell your brain that you can do it.

THE HEALING POWER OF VISUALIZATION
In recent years, a big debate has begun about whether visualization can help "heal" people who are sick, specifically breast cancer patients. According to the Breastcancer.org, studies have shown that visualization or guided imagery have temporarily increased immune system function to keep

the rest of the body healthy, help reduce feelings of depression, and increase feelings of well-being.[84] The organization's website describes a "technique in which a person imagines pictures, sounds, smells, and other sensations associated with reaching a goal. Imagining being in a certain environment or situation can activate the senses, producing a physical or psychological effect."[85]

You can practice these sessions either at home or with a trained therapist, and they take on average twenty to thirty minutes. A typical session looks a lot like how Ashanti practices visualization. According to the website, they begin with the therapist guiding your imagination to a place in your mind where you feel safe, relaxed, and comfortable[86] Here they will create an atmosphere so the patient is not distracted by their surroundings and remains focused on the place in their mind. Once a clear mindset is established, the patient is asked to imagine one of two visualizations—either a Pac-Man-like character chasing and eating the cancer cells or a warm healing light over the place where the cancer is or was. Breastcancer.org studies in the United States, United Kingdom, and Korea all showed improvement in those practicing it. Their immune system function increased as anxiety, depression, and moodiness decreased. The guided imagery groups all showed improvements and experienced a better quality of life than those in the control groups not practicing it.[87]

---

84 "Guide Imagery," Breastcancer.org, accessed May 2, 2020.
85 Ibid.
86 Ibid.
87 Ibid.

The best part about this research is that it may apply to other diseases people are fighting. Anyone undergoing treatment for cancer or recovering can practice it in the comfort of their own home, and it is considered a safe practice. This relatively recent discovery shows how much we still don't know about our bodies and just how powerful the mind is. We have yet to understand its true potential and the full capability of visualization. It's incredible that something so simple as spending twenty or thirty minutes thinking quietly along with visualization can have such a significant impact on our bodies—an impact so powerful it can help the immune system.

LESSONS FROM THIS CHAPTER:

- The power of visualization is stronger than you may realize. Start using it to achieve your goals!

- Practice Ashanti's visualization technique once a week.

- Nothing is impossible if you believe it.

CHAPTER 11

YOUR DREAM CAN BE A REALITY

Ashanti Johnson is showing others how to change their mindsets and visualize to achieve their fitness goals. Mary Morrisey is showing others about the power of dreaming.

In a 365-day period, what would you love to say about what is happening in your life? Take a moment to think about that. Would you like to have graduated college and be beginning your first full-time job? Do you want to have run a marathon? Or maybe you would like to have a closer relationship with a sibling? Perhaps you are ready to take the next steps in your career.

Mary Morrisey, in her TED Talk "Dreams into Reality", said we long for greater freedom. "We feel a discontent with certain circumstances and situations. And if we just keep breathing for another 365 days, we will create results, because that is what humans do."[88]

---

[88] Mary Morrisey, "The Hidden Code for Transforming Dreams into Reality," YouTube, uploaded December 21, 2016, Video, 8.36, (1.11-1.23).

Mary explains that humans create results in four different areas—in health and well-being, relationships, vocation, and time and money. Mary stood on the stage dressed in a smart, red suit and questioned the audience: "In which of these areas would you like to create results, and what would they be?" She went on to state that life one year from this moment might seem so far away and difficult to even try to imagine, but in the long-term perspective, a year is not that long.

PUT IT IN PERSPECTIVE
I remember starting college and learning that I needed to complete 124 credits in order to graduate. With each class being worth about four credits each, the number of years spanning ahead that I'd need to spend with my nose in a textbook seemed endless. Yet now I am amazed by how quickly those years passed. When we think of time in chunks like weeks, months, or years, they seem vast and never-ending. But we have all experienced these periods passing quickly, wondering where the time went. Although thinking a year into the future may seem like a long time away to envision a window, I can assure you it is not.

HOW MARY BUILT A FIELD OF DREAMS
Forty years ago, when Mary was working on her undergraduate degree to become a teacher, she became interested in the idea of transformation, particularly in children. Her purpose at that point was to "help children discover a kind of self-esteem so no matter what their circumstance or their situations, they could actually believe they could become

the person they wanted to be and achieve the things they wanted to achieve."[89]

After getting her undergraduate degree, she earned a graduate degree in counseling psychology and an honorary doctorate. Her first book, *Building Your Field of Dreams*, became a PBS special. She also worked with the Dalai Lama for seven years. This involved three weeklong meetings. In her career, she also had conversations with world leaders discussing how global issues can be transformed.

Mary is an influential woman who has also spoken at the United Nations three times. One time she was accompanied by Martin Luther King, Jr.'s children and Gandhi's grandchildren to create a sixty-four-day season for nonviolence. They focused on teaching junior high children how to solve problems without violence and by caring for one another. She also worked with Nelson Mandela and got to ask him a burning question: "How do you transform your results?"

"That has been my quest and my interest and my deep longing so that I could transfer that [information] and offer that to the people I have had the privilege of working with. I've been honored to work with tens of thousands of people around the world around changing their results," Mary said.[90] However, she explained it doesn't mean that all dreams and all results work out the desired way.

Sometimes it doesn't pan out the way you wish, and that is natural and okay. Dreams and windows change as we evolve

---

89 Ibid, 2.55-3.24.

90 Ibid, 4.52-5.04.

and experience new things, but we can always have them and move one step closer to achieving them.

According to Mary, dream builders use three steps to transform their results, "so that the dream wins over conditions; so that the dream wins over time; so that the dreams win over all kinds of circumstances, situations, and even our history, no matter how it's been there."[91]

Mary refers to Henry David Thoreau, who spent two years, two months, and two days experimenting living in the woods to learn about a purposeful life and understand what life had to teach him. After his experiment, he wrote an essay, which today is extremely popular and quoted worldwide. One of Thoreau's quotes is, "If one advances confidently in the direction of his dreams, and endeavors to live the life which he has imagined, he will meet with a success unexpected in common hours."[92]

"This quote leads to the first thing that dream builders or people who evolve their results do,"[93] Mary affirmed. They all have an idea of what they want their life to be like. Having specific details of your dream will help you to be more likely to achieve it. For example, if you want to travel, where do you want to go? Is it the Caribbean, Italy, Norway, or Africa?

Everyone in the TED Talk audience may be considering traveling to the United States, but each destination, each city is

---

91   Ibid, 5.36-5.57.

92   "A Quote from Walden," Goodreads, accessed May 31, 2020.

93   Mary Morrisey, "The Hidden Code for Transforming Dreams into Reality," YouTube, uploaded December 21, 2016, Video, 8.36, (6.58-7.05).

very different. Mary also warned not to think about what you can do, but what you love. Put yourself first rather than worrying about external factors. What does your soul crave?

Being at the beginning of my adult life, I have been asking myself this question a lot recently: what does my soul crave? It is an exciting but also a nerve-wracking stage of life to be in, but the beauty of it right now is that it is the perfect time to think about my dreams with little responsibilities holding me back. However, I am a firm believer that if you find yourself unhappy and not on the pathway to achieving your dreams, at any point in life, something should be changed. You need to start looking through a different window. You need to reimagine the curtains and the window frame along with the view you are seeking.

MARY'S STORY

When Mary was in her junior year of high school, she got pregnant and married the father of her child. Her principal expelled her and made her go to another school to complete her senior year. Mary recalled the school was for "delinquent boys and pregnant girls."[94]

A few months later, Mary was diagnosed with fatal kidney disease. One of her kidneys was destroyed, and the other was 50 percent destroyed. Told by doctors she only had six months left to live if they performed a successful surgery to reduce the blood toxin level, life looked bleak and scary with a newborn baby. The night before her surgery in the hospital, a pastor offered to pray for her. Mary responded, "Well, maybe."

---

94 Ibid, 9.08-9.16.

Mary explained everything that had happened to her recently. The pastor then told her that "everything is created twice. Everything around you first had to be a thought before it became a thing."[95] She then asked Mary if perhaps she hated herself, which was manifesting as physical punishment to her body, without realizing it. "Is it possible a correlation exists between thoughts and our physical beings?" the pastor questioned. She gave Mary a new perspective for both thinking and emotion. The pastor asked if she thought she could have the surgery and then fully recover. She went on to ask, if there are infinite numbers of possibilities, is that not one? Mary believed the pastor and focused on the possibility that her body would heal rather than die.

To the doctor's amazement, a few months later at a check-up, Mary was more than okay. Six months after her surgery when her time on Earth should have been up, the opposite had occurred. Her numbers had improved, and much to the doctor's surprise, it looked like she would fully recover.

This was Mary's inspiration to study the transformation of results because, unconsciously, her mind was making her body sicker. When the toxic thoughts left her mind, her body healed and she became well again. Anytime toxic thoughts started to creep into her mind, she said, "No, that left with a kidney." She reminded herself that she wanted to be a teacher and be there for her son. She envisioned walking her five-year-old son into kindergarten for the first time or sitting at his wedding while he married the love of his life. Each time

---

95 Ibid, 10.33-11.03.

she pushed away the toxic thoughts, instead dreaming and thinking forward for the future.

FOCUS ON YOUR DREAMS

"After forty-five years of studying, and relating to tens of thousands of people, I know these three things," she said. "The first one is to create with clarity, have a specific dream. The clearer the dream you can design, the more your brain can work on that frequency," she said, relating this explanation to fine-tuning a radio to get the right signal. "The second one is to refuse to stay discouraged. We all get discouraged at some point, but refuse to remain feeling like that in order to achieve your dream. The last one is to be more interested in growth than comfort. Grow to service your dream. Don't stay in your comfort zone, because you won't grow as a person. Discomfort pushes our boundaries and character just a little more, helping us in the long run."[96]

Mary has opened the doors to me for a whole new perspective. Her TED Talk and story have allowed me to reflect and question my daily attitude toward life. Do I have clarity about my dreams? Am I making steps toward achieving them and stepping outside my comfort zone enough? Once you know your dreams, it makes it easier to take steps toward achieving them. We can learn a lot from Mary. We can achieve our dreams by visualizing just like Dr. G, Ashanti, and Mary did. Growth, faith, and belief live in Mary's story. We all need to believe that we can achieve our dreams; that is the first step to making them a reality.

---

96   Ibid, 15.48-18.28.

LESSONS FROM THIS CHAPTER:

- Always have a dream!

- Listen to what will make your soul happy.

- Create a clear dream that is easy to visualize.

- Do not be discouraged when it feels out of reach. You will get there!

- Keep growing. Keep stepping outside your comfort zone. Keep progressing.

CHAPTER 12

THE MAGIC BEGINS IN PENCILS

———

Practicing visualization techniques like Mary Morrisey is not the only way to envision your future and achieve your dreams. Patti Dobrowolski is an internationally acclaimed keynote and three-time TEDx speaker, multiple business award winner, and past Broadway performer. In her talks, she explores drawing the future and what happens when an individual takes a pen to paper and sketches out his or her dreams.

I am a very visual person. Whenever I study, I know I need to handwrite notes or draw little diagrams next to certain concepts. I wish I didn't have to go through that long process to study, but it is worth it. I like color and shapes in my notes rather than listening or reading to the lecture. So when I learned about this technique as a possibility to achieve goals and dreams, I got excited to learn more.

"A solitary fantasy can transform a million realities,"[97] Patti said, quoting Mary Angelou at the beginning of her TED Talk, "Draw Your Future."[98] Just as Mary Morrisey explained in the previous chapter, having a clear dream rather than a vague one can lead you closer to your goal.

COULD YOU BE PART OF THE 9:1 RATIO?

Patti walked onto the stage with her short, white punk-styled hair and black-rimmed glasses. She was wearing a business casual blazer and trousers with a yellow-luminescent blouse underneath. She immediately gave the impression of being bold, and she proved it when she said, "The odds are nine to one of someone changing his or her behavior for that person's dreams to come true." Therefore, few people achieve the ultimate goal of achieving their vision or dream. If we put ten readers of this book into a metaphorical room, only one of those readers would actually believe in his or her dreams enough to start changing behavior to make them come true.

Every year, I am sure we all make at least one new year's resolution. This will be the year we finally get healthy and fit. This will be the year we finally quit our jobs and find our dream jobs. This will be the year we do that monthlong road trip and see the wonders of the world. How many of us actually start making changes on January 2 to achieve our resolution? Very few of us, including myself. How many of us after one month even achieve our goal? Even fewer. Why

---

97 "A Quote from Poems," Goodreads, accessed June 2, 2020.
98 Patti Dobrowolski, "Draw Your Future," filmed January 10, 2012 at TEDxRainier, video, 10.34.

can't we stay consistent and put one foot in front of the other to make a change? I have been asking myself this for years as, annually, I fail to reach my New Year's resolutions.

Patti believes there are three steps to beating the 9:1 statistic of not making a change. Think about this for a second. Patti has found a way for us to start making a change to allow us to achieve our goals!

You must:

- Have the ability to see it.

- Believe it can happen.

- Ask and train your brain to work toward making a change to achieve it.

According to Healthline, on average, "It takes sixty-six days to make a behavior a habit."[99] So if you need to change a habit, such as not snacking at night or reading the news in the morning, you must do it for sixty-six days consistently to make it happen.

But how do we see our visions turn into realities? People like Ashanti Johnson have suggested using mindfulness. We know Ashanti believes that if we can enter a calm state of mind by imagining ourselves to be in our safe places, then, in our mind's eye, we create and imagine the vision. We can place ourselves

---

99 "How Long Does It Actually Take To Form A New Habit?," *Healthline*, accessed May 8 2020.

in a position to feel, see, and smell everything surrounding us. In return, we trick our brains into believing that what is happening is real rather than us exploring our imagination.

WHY YOU SHOULD GET YOUR PENCILS OUT

Patti, however, suggests another way to think about our futures to vision our dreams—drawing. This made me think of the old saying, "A picture is worth a thousand words."[100] But is drawing our visions and dreams more effective than thinking of them in our mind's eye?

Patti recalled a time when the president of Roche Pharmaceuticals asked all the employees to create a picture of the company's vision in which the mission is reflected.[101] Before the exercise, employees were asked if they knew the mission and vision of the company. Surprisingly, fewer than 40 percent understood the company's vision and strategy. However, after the exercise, 96 percent understood the vision and the strategy of the company. Shockingly, 84 percent now understood the reasoning behind what they did every day.

These statistics improved dramatically just through the exercise of drawing. The results illustrate that by putting a pen to paper, we can help the brain process and understand information. It seems that after this exercise, the employees understood their workplace on a deeper level, which probably

---

100 Gary Martin, "'A Picture Is Worth A Thousand Words' - The Meaning And Origin Of This Phrase," *Phrasefinder,* accessed June 2, 2020.

101 Patti Dobrowolski, "Draw Your Future," filmed January 10, 2012 at TEDxRainier, video, 10.34. (2.07-2.30)

meant their work, along with their connection to the company and its mission, improved.

According to Pam Mueller of Princeton University, when students type their notes, they tend not to filter, summarize, and paraphrase what they are learning.[102] Rather, they type everything they hear, which is different from students who write their notes. Students who handwrite notes spend longer on the information, processing it, and filtering what to write on the paper.[103] This extra time generally benefits the student even if they have less information on the page compared to the student who typed the lecture. Some of my classes at university banned us from using laptops (unless needed through disability services) to take our notes. The professor believed we performed better when writing instead of typing.

I agree with Pam Mueller. From a student's perspective, I remember and process my notes better when they are written as compared to typed. A computer screen with words and bullet points all start to look the same to me. However, when I can handwrite notes, designing the layout with color and doodles on the page, they stand out to me, and I remember the information on the page better.

TIME TO GET CREATIVE

Patti explained how everyone should get a blank piece of paper to draw out their vision and road map to change.[104]

---

102   NPR Choice Page," *National Public Radio,* accessed May 8, 2020.

103   Ibid.

104   Patti Dobrowolski, "Draw Your Future," filmed January 10, 2012 at TEDxRainier, video, 10.34, (2.40-3.05).

The left side should be titled "current state" and the right side titled "desired new reality." As the "artist," we can then see the difference in the two sides and determine how to move from the state on the left side to the right.

Patti used the example of a fictional man named Joe to draw out a vision for the TED Talk audience. She stood next to a giant piece of blank paper and started sketching out the stick figure man-of-the-night. The audience learned that in Joe's current state, he has a good job, a wife named Amy, and he earns good money. But Joe wants more in his life. He finds his job difficult, which is extra miserable when the boss is mean. He spends every day living and believing he has a higher purpose in his life, but he is unsure of what that is and if it is possible to reach one day.

"Drawing out our thinking process tricks the logical left side of our brains into thinking that we aren't taking it seriously. This then allows us to engage with the right side of our brain, the creative side."[105]

On the other side, Patti sketched out a much happier looking Joe. His face is beaming as he sits in a different office where he is the boss. Joe is bursting with creativity, and he finally feels like he has reached his purpose, along with being free and full of love. The audience and Patti love this new and improved version of Joe.

PAINT THE PICTURE
When I was sixteen and studying for my GSCE biology exam, I had to know the diagram of a heart. Overwhelmed with

---

105 Ibid, 4.16-4.37.

information and key words and definitions, I was unsure how I would remember all the details. My teacher told us to draw out a diagram and label it. To this day, over five years later, I can still label a diagram of a heart because I remember the diagram and the colors that I once drew so perfectly. That drawing, along with the information, has stuck with me, proving our brains are more capable than we realize.

"We remember things better when they are attached to a picture—65 percent better, to be exact," according to Patti.[106] Thoughts can be so easy to forget, which is why many of us, including myself, write things down. Like many others, every day I make a list of everything I need to do. When we draw and make it physically visible, it makes whatever we are trying to remember easier to remember. However, you must be the one to draw the picture; otherwise, it won't have the same impact. "You get the most power when you paint your own picture," Patti said.[107]

Once your picture is drawn, the next step is to fill the picture with color and emotion. Our brains release serotonin and oxytocin when we dream and draw. Therefore, this process will also make us feel happy, capable of achieving, creative, and overall cool, Patti explained to the audience as she colored in the drawings of Joe, making everything look brighter.

"Here's where the magic begins. Your brain knows you. It's cataloged everything you've seen, heard, experienced—real

---

[106] Ibid, 3.48-3.55.
[107] Ibid, 5.39-5.43.

or imaginary. You just have to ask it to put the pieces together for you. It's as simple as that," Patti assured.[108]

It's like our brain is one big puzzle trying to jumble all the pieces together. When we draw, our brain is finally putting the pieces of the puzzle together. We can see it laid out in front of us, and it makes sense rather than being a collection of sporadic pieces in random places.

Once you have the color in the drawing, the final step is to look at the picture you have created and then close your eyes. Closing your eyes allows the brain to recycle what it sees. It will then reconstruct, add, and serve a solution. But this will only happen when you are relaxed. So the best way to complete this exercise is to draw and think all together because you will still have serotonin and oxytocin in your system.

So the three steps Patti mentioned are see it, believe it, and act on it.

BE BOLD, HONEST, AND CREATIVE
"How can you get yourself to the boldest thing? By drawing the most compelling picture. So when you look here (Patti pointed to the side labeled 'current state'), you're in pain. It hurts. And when you're here (Patti pointed to the side labeled 'desired new reality'), you're ecstatic."[109]

---

108 Ibid, 6.47-7.01.

109 Ibid, 8.49-8.58.

Think of all the pictures you have seen over the years, whether they are drawn, photographed, painted, or sketched. Which ones inspired an emotion? Whether it is a sad one that brings a pain to your chest or a lump to your throat or a happy one that you can't help but smile at, the drawings you create from this exercise have the same power. They have even more power because you created them, and, therefore, it is personal to you and you only. That emotion will kick-start your journey to achieving your goal!

Patti said you should get up and look at that picture every day. Frame it. Pin it on the fridge. Put it as your phone lock screen. Just find a way to see it every day. Step into the possibility of it happening by taking small steps. The more you take, the bigger the reality becomes. That is how you become the one in nine to making a change happen, to be one step closer to achieving your dreams.

LESSONS FROM THIS CHAPTER:
- Use visualization techniques to envision your future.
- Draw your future with pen and paper.
- When we put pen to paper, our brain remembers better!
- Use color and emotion when drawing your vision.
- Put your drawing somewhere visible to see it every day.

CHAPTER 13

OPRAH WINFREY AND VISION BOARDS

Another visualization method similar to Patti Dobrowolskis's idea of drawing is using a vision board or a dream board. The difference between drawing and a vision board is that you collect images and text rather than hand-create it.

Vision boards are typically poster-sized and contain images and text of the goals a person wants to achieve. Both techniques include seeing images on paper as inspiration. Physically creating something often inspires the drive to want to make a change compared to seeing it in your mind's eye and practicing mindfulness. A vision board uses multiple images collaged together to represent numerous goals or mini goals.

In a 2018 press interview for her new movie, *A Wrinkle in Time*, Oprah discussed using vision boards along with her costar, Reese Witherspoon, and the interviewer, Jaleesa

Lashay. Oprah said she no longer uses them, as she is now a powerful manifester, but Reese said she still does.[110] It turns out the young interviewer included meeting Oprah on her vision board that year. When hearing this, Oprah smiled from ear to ear, getting up from her chair and engulfing the interviewer in a big hug. She looked so pleased as she congratulated her for reaching a goal she had envisioned.

I love this story because these three women are sharing something very raw and authentic; two of them are big stars, but they are all bonding over something they practice, believe in, and manifest. Not only that but they are celebrating reaching a goal together, knowing that vision boards can create this power. I enjoyed most that this moment was unplanned and unscripted—just three women sharing something and celebrating all because of one thing they have in common.

Oprah shared advice in the interview on how to create a vision board: "You have to meet the vibration. You can't be above or below it.... In order to draw the thing to you that you want to come, you can't want it so much that you fear that you won't get it. You have to want it. So in order for me to be on your [Jaleesa's] vision board, you must have put it there and let it go, and then you weren't thinking about it every day because it doesn't come to you that way. You have to do it and put it there. You have to meet that

---

110 BlackTreeTV, "Oprah Gives a Master Class on Manifestation and Vision Boards - *A Wrinkle in Time*," uploaded March 8, 2018, YouTube video, 4:21, (0.01-1.09).

vibration. You have to prepare yourself to be there and be ready when it shows up."[111]

Oprah's statement, "You can't want it so much that you fear you won't get it; you have to want it,"[112] speaks volumes. Often, when we really want something, we get scared for fear of rejection or just never achieving it. For example, suppose you want your driver's license. You've been thinking about it since you were fifteen. Now you have the chance to take the test, but you are scared that something will go wrong and you will be left sitting in the car with "FAIL" written on your permit. That fear can manifest itself so you never go to the DMV and take the test. But if you want it, if you truly want it, you must make that appointment and sit in that line to drive away with the examiner. We all know how fear can hold us back, but you must not let this happen if you want to achieve your goal. You must embrace stepping outside of your comfort zone.

According to *Psychology Today*, studies have shown that our thoughts are instructions for actions. Therefore "mental imagery impacts many cognitive processes in the brain: motor control, attention, perception, planning, and memory. So the brain is getting trained for actual performance during visualization. It's been found that mental practices can enhance motivation, increase confidence and self-efficacy, improve motor performance, prime your brain for success, and increase states of flow—all relevant to achieving your best life!"[113]

---

[111] Ibid, 1.45-2.16.

[112] Ibid, 1.55-1.58.

[113] AJ Adams, "Seeing is Believing: The Power of Visualization," *Psychology Today,* uploaded December 03, 2009.

Celebrities aren't the only ones practicing visualization. Sports teams and athletes have been doing it for decades.[114] Athletes and whole teams will often visualize a game or a tournament before running onto the field or stepping onto the court. The visualization includes everything from imagining the place you will be, to what your senses feel like when in that particular place, to the individual's knowledge of the sport. The athletes play it in their minds as they walk through each moment step by step to visualize what will happen. In fact, one of the world's greatest athletes, Muhammad Ali, often used mental practices before going into the rings, such as "affirmation; visualization; mental rehearsal; self-confirmation; and perhaps the most powerful epigram of personal worth ever uttered: 'I am the greatest.'"[115]

Anyone who has played a sport can tell you a story of when they used their mind over matter. When I was younger, I used to sprint competitively for my school. I remember the sensation of running and wanting to give up mid-race, but instead, I'd visualize crossing the finish line, using that image as my driving force. My legs burned as I neared the last few meters of the race. My chest stung from pumping in breath, and the wind whipped against my face as I pushed my body harder and harder. Everything inside of me wanted to stop. But I didn't. Do you know why? It's because I kept thinking about that finish line. I kept thinking about my teammates counting on me. I kept thinking about my mum and sister intently watching me, cheering on every step. The

---

114 Ibid.

115 Ibid.

visualization of crossing the finish line kept every inch of my body moving toward it.

CREATING A VISION BOARD

So how do you make a vision board? Information online, including from YouTube videos, articles, and multiple books, provides a multitude of advice and guidelines. But here is my guide from what Oprah illustrated.

- First, you need to enjoy some arts and crafts and, of course, have goals that you want to achieve.[116] A vision board is not to be confused with a mood board. A mood board is used to create an idea about aesthetics when planning to decorate or throw a party, for example, but a vision board is about getting inspiration to achieve goals. It is not all about materialistic goals either; it should be focused on how you want to feel.

- When creating a vision board, set the tone around you.[117] Although you want it to be fun and pretty to look at later, it is also a time to be thinking deeply and feeling relaxed. Turn off all potential distractions and clear your head before starting. Work in a space that you find relaxing. Why not put on your favorite music and indulge in your favored snacks when you create it?

---

116 Brigitt Earley, "Here's How Make a Vision Board," *The Oprah Magazine*, uploaded November 26, 2019.

117 Ibid.

- When your goals are chosen, the next part is to start creating.[118] Gather magazines, print images from Instagram and Pinterest, and look through your pictures. Use text also and maybe include some quotes as inspiration. Each vision board is individual to the person and their goals, but keeping it less cluttered and more aesthetically pleasing will make the board look more attractive and pleasing to the eye. In return, you are drawing your attention to it each time you see it.

- The next step is to hang it in a place where you'll often see it.[119] It could be by your desk, in your bedroom, or even opposite the toilet as long as you will look at it frequently to remind yourself of what you want. However, you don't want the reminder to be overwhelming. If this becomes the case, relocate the board or create smaller vision boards.

This reminds me of a study technique I was taught before taking my GCSE exams at the age of sixteen. We were told to put Post-it notes and cue cards around our house and our bedroom. That way when we walked into the kitchen and went to the snack cupboard, we'd discover a card explaining Pythagoras just inside the door. Then when we took the test and needed the equation for Pythagoras, we'd visualize walking into the kitchen and opening up the snack cupboard to see the card. Putting vision boards in frequently used locations will subconsciously do the same thing as study cards do for students. You will frequently see them, and the

---

118 Ibid.

119 Ibid.

image will slowly burn into your memory. It will no longer become something you created, but it will become part of you.

As humans, our ideas always change and evolve as we have new experiences and interact with others. So don't be afraid to make changes to your vision and alter it! The world is always changing day to day, and so are you. It is only natural if a vision board also begins to evolve and change. Make adjustments when you feel it is necessary to do so and change things around. Take images and quotes off, replacing them with new goals. If you want, restart it from scratch. But never be sad that the goal you set within a specific time didn't get achieved. It is never too late to keep reaching for the goal, as long as you keep moving.

LESSONS FROM THIS CHAPTER:
- Vision boards allow creativity for ideas that can be easily changed and replaced.

- Physical visualization makes it easier to envision your goals.

- Oprah loved to practice visualization and it bought her much success, so it is worth a try!

CONCLUSION

THE FINAL OVERVIEW
We can find our mirrors in many places. It may be a family member, friend, peer, professor, boss, speaker, or a celebrity. When we open ourselves to new experiences by stepping outside of our comfort zones, we are likely to meet new people and, in return, meet new mirrors. Likewise, when we find ourselves in a time of change, whether that is starting a new job or moving to a new apartment, we shouldn't be scared, as change brings good.

We can envision and look through our windows in many ways, whether by spending fifteen minutes a day in a quiet place to create the vision in our mind, drawing it out on a piece of paper using splashes of color, or creating a vision board with a collage of images and quotes. The view from our window may change over time as we have new experiences, growing and altering our goals. But as long as we keep the curtains drawn back and continue to look out of our windows, we can remain focused on our vision.

By refocusing the way we think through the concept of mirrors and windows, I believe we can view success in a new way. No longer does success, for whatever goal, need to be overwhelming or seemingly unreachable. By using mirrors and windows, we can reach our goals.

Hopefully, the success stories of the empowering women I have shared in this book have shown that no matter who you are, what your background is, or how much money you may have or not have, if you believe in yourself and practice looking through your window, you can achieve anything.

I wrote this book because I wanted to share with others what I have learned about the importance of mentors and the power of visualization. If we can change the way we think and what we think, it opens up endless possibilities that can be achieved. We can make our dreams a reality.

I shared stories from women because I wanted to show that in a male-dominated world, women are breaking through and achieving their dreams. The world is changing now more than ever before with increasing numbers of female leaders throughout different industries.

THE DISCOVERY PROCESS

This book started by looking at the importance of change and stepping outside of comfort zones. If we are stagnant, nothing new will ever grow and we will never achieve our dreams or turn them into realities. Change is inevitable, and 2020 has proven to everyone just how quickly change can happen—an important lesson for us all.

We met Aidyl Gonzalez-Serricchio (Dr. G), who inspired her students to follow their dreams in STEM and created a mirror for others to look at through their windows. She entered the field with no mirrors or windows that reflected someone like her. Now others look up to her as a role model and identify with her.

Sheryl Sandberg is using her prominent position as COO at Facebook to help thousands of other women to lean in to achieve their dreams and work toward creating an equal world for men and women in the workplace.

Susan O'Day taught us to be confident with ourselves and know our potential. If you know what you want, demand it. She also taught us to never limit ourselves because we never know what we might achieve.

Gay Cook showed us the importance of mirrors and how networking can lead to amazing opportunities that can shape careers. Part of using mirrors and windows is trusting the process. It may not always be crystal clear during the moment, but know that it is leading you one step closer.

Jackie Spencer proved to us the importance of following our hearts to do something that makes us happy. Even when she didn't have a specific window to look through, she believed in her goals and learned from her mirrors to be where she is today.

Susan Santner showed us how we can help others by being their mirror. She also showed us how we can help others to fulfill their goals in their windows.

Debra Benton taught us the importance of having multiple mentors of all ages and how it can benefit not only us but other mentors too.

Judith Heumann showed us how when we keep focusing on envisioning our window, we can achieve anything we want, whether it be a big or little change.

Then we explored the different ways we can practice envisioning to look through our windows. We can create the vision in our mind like Ashanti Johnson. We can draw it out on a piece of paper like Patti Dobrowolski. Or we can create a vision board like Oprah Winfrey and Reese Witherspoon. Finally, Mary Morrisey taught us about the importance of having clarity in our dreams in order to achieve them.

Observing all these stories confirmed how by using both mirrors and windows, we can unlock a new way to envision our success. I believed in this concept from the start. However, I was pleasantly surprised at the results and how these success stories illustrated what could happen if we practice combining mirrors and windows.

THE PERSONAL SIDE
Being at a crossroads in my life, with so much change and many opportunities to go in any direction, has been a privilege that students easily forget they have. However, it is also overwhelming, scary, and daunting.

Writing this book, I have deeply learned about mirrors and windows and feel lighter and less overwhelmed and scared. I hope if you are in a similar position, you do too. I now fully understand that I have the power to design my dreams, building them with clarity and purpose, to then manifest them into my reality. Just like you, I can draw whatever I want on the other side of my window and keep looking out at the view.

I also now understand the importance of not only having mentors but building relationships with them. I can combine this along with taking opportunities to network, network, network, because you never know who you will meet and how they may impact your life.

Writing this book has been an emotional journey, not just from reflecting on myself but physically creating it. The hours of work, perseverance, and dedication have given me a whole new perspective and respect for authors and creators. I wholeheartedly enjoyed the process of discovering and learning and creating mirrors along the way that I will forever remember.

A CALL TO ACTION
Whatever chapter of life you may be in, whether high school, university, starting a career, changing your career, or achieving a dream or goal, I hope you will finish this book having learned something new that you can practice in everyday life.

I hope you have been inspired, encouraged to embrace change, challenged to set new goals and achieve them, readied to mirror the success of others, and persuaded to practice envisioning in day-to-day life. I hope it has opened you to new insights that will improve your mindset.

Lastly, I want you to create mirrors for yourself to look into and windows for yourself to look out to, unlocking your new way to envision your success.

APPENDIX

INTRODUCTION:
Abbajay, Mary. "Mentoring Matters: Three Essential Elements of Success." Forbes Magazine. Jan 20, 2019,11:52 a.m. EST.
https://www.forbes.com/sites/maryabbajay/2019/01/20/mentoring-matters-three-essential-element-of-success/#1856df0645a9.

Stringer, Heather. "The life-changing power of mentors." American Psychological Association 47, no.6. (June 2016): 54.
https://www.apa.org/monitor/2016/06/mentors.

CHAPTER 1:
"A Comfort Zone Is a Beautiful Place, But Nothing Ever Grows There (With Images) | Comfort Zone Quotes, Boxing Quotes, Life Quotes." Pinterest. Accessed May 18, 2020.
https://www.pinterest.com/pin/562950022154180411/.

Berman, Rachel. "Super Deep Disney Quotes | Movies." Oh My Disney. Accessed May 17, 2020.
https://ohmy.disney.com/movies/2013/05/08/super-deep-disney-quotes/.

"Hattie McDaniel." IMDB. Accessed May 17, 2020.
https://www.imdb.com/name/nm0567408/awards?ref_=nm_awd.

"Malala Fund | Working for a World Where All Girls Can Learn and Lead." Malala. Org. Accessed May 17, 2020.
https://www.malala.org/.

Proudfoot, Jenny. "The 100 Most Inspirational Women of The Last 100 Years." Marie Claire. Uploaded March 5, 2020, 4:53 PM.
https://www.marieclaire.co.uk/news/most-inspirational-women-575925.

Spector, Nicole. "Why We Find Change So Difficult, According to Neuroscience." NBC News. Uploaded November 12, 2018, 5:07 a.m. PST.
https://www.nbcnews.com/better/health/how-train-your-brain-accept-change-according-neuroscience-ncna934011.

"The Nobel Peace Prize 2014." Nobelprize.Org. Accessed May 17, 2020.
https://www.nobelprize.org/prizes/peace/2014/yousafzai/biographical/.

CHAPTER 2:
Mariel Padilla. "First All-Female Spacewalk Is Back On, Nasa Says." The New York Times. Uploaded October 5, 2019.
https://www.nytimes.com/2019/10/05/science/NASA-female-spacewalk.html.

"Project Possum | The Possum 13." Project Possum. Accessed May 31, 2020.
https://projectpossum.org/the-possum-13/.

Stem Education Data. "Has the Employment of Women and Minorities in S&E Jobs Increased?" Accessed April 24, 2020.
https://nsf.gov/nsb/sei/edTool/data/workforce-07.html.

CHAPTER 3:
Forbes. "#1415 Sheryl Sandberg." Accessed April 23, 2020.
https://www.forbes.com/profile/sheryl-sandberg/#40c567d258b6.

Lean In. "About the Org." Accessed April 23, 2020.
https://leanin.org/about

Rothschild, Mike. "Female Presidents Currently in Office." Ranker. May 24, 2019.
https://www.ranker.com/list/women-presidents/mike-rothschild.

Sandberg, Sheryl. "Why We Have Too Few Women Leaders." TED. December 21, 2010. Video, 15.28.
https://www.youtube.com/watch?v=18uDutylDa4.

CHAPTER 4:
Gillenwater, Sharon. "2018's State of Women CIOs in the Fortune 500." Boardroom Insiders. Accessed April 23, 2020.
https://web.boardroominsiders.com/the-state-of-women-cios-in-2016.

"Home – Alliance for Social Innovation," Alliance for So Cal Innovation. Accessed May 23. 2020.
https://www.alliancesocal.org/home.

Zillman, Claire. "The Fortune 500 Has More Female CEOs Than Ever Before." Fortune. Accessed April 23, 2020.
https://fortune.com/2019/05/16/fortune-500-female-ceos/.

CHAPTER 5:
DeSilver, Drew. "A Record Number of Women Will Be Serving in the New Congress." Pew Research Center. Accessed April 25, 2020.
https://www.pewresearch.org/fact-tank/2018/12/18/record-number-women-in-congress/.

Goodreads. "A Quote by Marilyn Monroe." Accessed April 25, 2020.
https://www.goodreads.com/quotes/12379-i-believe-that-everything-happens-for-a-reason-people-change.

International Women's Forum. "About Us Overview." Accessed April 25, 2020.
https://www.iwforum.org/about_us_overview.

MSU Denver. "About MSU Denver." Accessed April 25, 2020.
https://www.msudenver.edu/about/.

Young, Jeffrey R. 2020. "How Many Times Will People Change Jobs? The Myth of the Endlessly-Job-Hopping Millennial." Edsurge. Uploaded July 20, 2017.
https://www.edsurge.com/news/2017-07-20-how-many-times-will-people-change-jobs-the-myth-of-the-endlessly-job-hopping-millennial.

CHAPTER 6:
"Beatles Heritage in Liverpool and Its Economics and Its Cultural Sector Impact: A Report for Liverpool City Council." Accessed May 24, 2020.
http://researchonline.ljmu.ac.uk/id/eprint/2900/1/Beatles%20Heritage%20in%20Liverpool%2048pp%20210x210mm%20aw.pdf.

Jackie Spencer BeatleGuide. "Tours." Accessed April 27, 2020.
https://www.jackiespencerbeatleguide.com/tours.html.

Marinucci, Steve. "1958 Liverpool Police Film Believed to Feature Earliest Glimpse of the Beatles." The Hollywood Reporter. March 9, 2017. 4:54 p.m. PST.
https://www.hollywoodreporter.com/news/1958-liverpool-police-film-believed-feature-earliest-glimpse-beatles-985001.

CHAPTER 7:
Bernstein, Sandra. "Being Present." Nursing 49, no. 6 (June 2019): 14-17.
https://journals.lww.com/nursing/Fulltext/2019/06000/Being_present__Mindfulness_and_nursing_practice.4.aspx.

Boyle, Patrick. "More Women Than Men Are Enrolled in Medical School." AAMC. Accessed April 29, 2020.
https://www.aamc.org/news-insights/more-women-men-are-enrolled-medical-school.

"National Nursing Workforce Study. NCSBN." NCSBN. Accessed April 29, 2020.
https://www.ncsbn.org/workforce.htm.

Online, Carson-Newman University. "25 Nursing Trends We Expect to See in 2020." Carson-Newman A Christian University. Uploaded January 6, 2020.
https://onlinenursing.cn.edu/news/nursing-trends.

CHAPTER 8:
"Executive Coach, Keynote Speaker, and Bestselling Author Debra Benton," Debra Benton. Accessed April 30, 2020.
https://www.debrabenton.com/.

"Senior Mentors: How to Connect with a Mentoring Project That Makes a Difference." Sunrise Senior Living. Accessed May 26, 2020.
https://www.sunriseseniorliving.com/blog/january-2019/senior-mentors-how-to-connect-with-a-mentoring-project-that-makes-a-difference.aspx.

Schumer, Lizz. "Why Mentoring Matters, and How to Get Started." New York Times. Uploaded September 26, 2018.
https://www.nytimes.com/2018/09/26/smarter-living/why-mentoring-matters-how-to-get-started.html.

CHAPTER 9:
Goodreads. "A Quote by Marilyn Monroe." Accessed April 25, 2020.
https://www.goodreads.com/quotes/12379-i-believe-that-everything-happens-for-a-reason-people-change.

Grim, Andrew. "Sitting-In for Disability Rights: The Section 504 Protests of the 1970s." National Museum of American History. Uploaded July 8, 2015.
https://americanhistory.si.edu/blog/sitting-disability-rights-section-504-protests-1970s.

Heumann, Judith. "Our Fight for Disability Rights – and Why We're Not Done Yet." Ted.com. March 2018. Video, 17.02.
https://www.ted.com/talks/judith_heumann_our_fight_for_disability_rights_and_why_we_re_not_done_yet.

"Judith Heumann 100 Women of the Year." TIME. March 5, 2020.
https://time.com/5793652/judith-heumann-100-women-of-the-year/.

Malcolm, Andrew H. "Woman in Wheelchair Sues to Become Teacher." New York Times. May 27, 1970.
https://www.nytimes.com/1970/05/27/archives/woman-in-wheel-chair-sues-to-become-teacher.html.

ONE. "12 Women Who Changed the World." Uploaded March 6, 2020.
https://www.one.org/us/blog/12-women-who-changed-the-world/.

CHAPTER 10:
"Guided Imagery." Breastcancer.org. Accessed May 2, 2020.
https://www.breastcancer.org/treatment/comp_med/types/imagery.

Johnson, Ashanti. "The Power of Visualization." YouTube. Uploaded May 16, 2018. Video, 15.43.
https://www.youtube.com/watch?v=S95-9-VuBoU.

CHAPTER 11:
"A Quote from Walden." Goodreads. Accessed May 31, 2020.
https://www.goodreads.com/quotes/290603-if-one-advances-confidently-in-the-direction-of-his-dreams.

Morrisey, Mary. "The Hidden Code for Transforming Dreams into Reality." YouTube. Uploaded December 21, 2016. Video, 18.36.
https://www.youtube.com/watch?v=UPoTsudFF4Y.

CHAPTER 12:
"A Quote from Poems." Goodreads. Accessed June 2, 2020.
https://www.goodreads.com/quotes/5483-if-one-is-lucky-a-solitary-fantasy-can-totally-transform.

Dobrowolski, Patti. "Draw Your Future." YouTube. Uploaded January 10, 2012 at TEDxRainier. Video. 10.34.
https://www.youtube.com/watch?v=zESeeaFDVSw.

"How Long Does It Actually Take to Form a New Habit?" Accessed May 8, 2020. Healthline. https://www.healthline.com/health/how-long-does-it-take-to-form-a-habit#base-figure.

Martin, Gary. "'A Picture Is Worth A Thousand Words' – The Meaning and Origin of This Phrase." Phrasefinder. Accessed June 2, 2020. https://www.phrases.org.uk/meanings/a-picture-is-worth-a-thousand-words.html.

"NPR Choice Page." Accessed May 8, 2020. Npr.org. https://www.npr.org/2016/04/17/474525392/attention-students-put-your-laptops-away.

CHAPTER 13:
Adams, AJ. "Seeing Is Believing: The Power of Visualization." Psychology Today. Uploaded December 03, 2009. https://www.psychologytoday.com/us/blog/flourish/200912/seeing-is-believing-the-power-visualization.

BlackTreeTV. "Oprah Gives a Master Class on Manifestation and Vision Boards – A Wrinkle in Time." Uploaded March 8, 2018. YouTube video. 4:21. https://www.youtube.com/watch?v=yHyh0BXqJ00.

Earley, Brigitt. "Here's How to Make a Vision Board." The Oprah Magazine. Uploaded November 26, 2019. https://www.oprahmag.com/life/a29959841/how-to-make-a-vision-board/.

ACKNOWLEDGMENTS

Thank you to all my interviewees who made my book a reality: Aidyl Gonzalez-Serricchio, Susan O'Day, Gay Cook, Jackie Spencer, Susan Santner, and Debra Benton. I really appreciate you taking the time to help me. In the process of learning and writing your chapters, each of you has become a mirror to me.

Thank you to my high school friends, Amy and Rachel, and thank you to my college friends, Thea, Brianna, and Kirstin, for your unending support and for sharing your excitement.

Thank you to New Degree Press, especially Eric Koester and Brian Bies, for giving me this opportunity to fulfill my childhood dream and helping me throughout the process. Thank you to Carol McKibben—I could not have done any of this without you.

Lastly, I'd also like to gratefully acknowledge those who believed in me before they even read a chapter:

Sarah Baker, Jon Baker, Beth Baker, Pauline West, Brandon Perry, Emma Clark, Peter Clark, Angie and Keith Francis,

Amy Malacalza, Rachel Beinus, Nicole Perry, Isabella Breda, Thea Holtlund, Kirstin Rosa, Brianna Zaragoza, Kayomi Kayoshi, Suman Chakraborty, Eric Koester, Taylor Ross, Francheska Cal, Lauren Good, James Evans, Abdulmalik Abdan, Tinathy Tran, Hanna Young, Blessy Pinzon, Randy Cantz, Aidyl Gonzalez-Serricchio, Nohemí Salazar, Sabrina Riggan, Susie Crayton, Nicole Kolde, Kari Schmitz, Madison Lyrenmann, Emma Hedges, Ana Paula González, Tamar Haddad, Elena Hotson, Oliver Roveda, Simone Goerlich, Peter Reinke, Taylor Campbell, Sofia Rojek, Terrence Yang, Chia-Li Chien, Josiah Gonzales, Jessica Reid, Jessica Bushman, Alexia Lee, and Malia Rorabaugh.

www.ingramcontent.com/pod-product-compliance
Lightning Source LLC
LaVergne TN
LVHW011837060526
838200LV00053B/4069